# How to Be a Moon

Embrace Your Worth.
Reflect God.
Light up Your Generation.

CARRYE BURR

ISBN-10: 0692148302
ISBN-13: 978-0692148303

# DEDICATION

This book is dedicated to my three beautiful children, Charlotte, Luke, and David. I'm in awe of how you reflect God in your own unique ways. You inspire me and give me so much joy.
I pray you become mesmerized by God's presence, know His purpose for you, and walk boldly to serve others in love.

I love you so much farther than the moon and back.

# CONTENTS

# ACKNOWLEDGMENTS

To my brave editors and writers' group, thank you for your time, friendship, and red-pens. The world thanks you for rescuing them from my mistakes.

To my prayer team, I'm beyond blessed to call each of you friend. Thank you for keeping me grounded in Jesus and for every powerful prayer for God's will to be done in this project.

To my launch team, you have blown me away in your encouragement and support. You helped me press on when it was hard to focus at the end, and gave me joy in a community of gifts. I can't thank you enough!

To my husband: I'm glad we could finally find a project where we agreed on symmetry. Thanks for creating another beautiful cover, but more importantly for walking me through all the emotions of book writing. Your support means more than you know. I love you.

To my long distance therapists (better known as Mom and Dad), thank you for every comment of encouragement, media tip, and kernel of wisdom you've passed along during these years of writing. You make me smile and I'm proud to be yours. Thank you for stretching me, listening well, and calling me deeper into God's heart.

Thank you to everyone who has shaped me over the years, inspired me to live beyond myself, and encouraged me to seek God first.
You taught me how to be a moon.

# INTRODUCTION

You've heard of the "crazy cat lady." Well, I'm the crazy moon lady. Nice to meet you.

I've been obsessed with the sky and all its accessories for as long as I can remember. As a teenager, when most girls were decorating with boy band posters, I painted my entire bedroom with celestial objects. The sun took up half of one wall, and my crescent moon, looking sadly like a banana, wrapped around one of my windows. My first tattoos were three bright stars on my foot, and as an adult, I purchased a "Luna" guitar with moon phases on the fretboard.

But I never imagined the moon had so many lessons to teach me.

In the last couple years, God's celestial creation turned unexpectedly into a classroom, revealing subtle lies I was believing about my value and my God. I realized my culture had turned the stars I loved into the ultimate symbol of worth. Stars are the people the world says we're supposed to follow, emulate, and aspire to be. If stars are valuable because of how bright they are, then shining is symbolic of our quest to know our value.

But being a star is a tricky business. According to our culture, stars must do more, be more, or be better than those around them to secure significance. Stars are little gassy balls of fire sputtering their hearts out to matter. I know because I've tried to shine on my own like a star. I've nearly exploded trying to make people happy, meet some unrealistic expectation of perfect morals, and accomplish enough to feel good about myself. Following star logic, I exhausted myself in comparison, competition, and approval seeking. As much as I love the idea of stars, I simply can't keep up with the world's definition.

But the moon is refreshingly different. The moon lights up the earth as the distant stars never could, yet it does so without creating any light of its own. No striving. No sputtering. And, thank God, no

1

gassiness. That moon just sits there, beautiful and content, confident in the sun it reflects.

And it occurred to me...that's how I want to live. I want to be content and confident, shining boldly in the dark without fear or striving. I don't want to spend so much of my life trying to shine that I'm not even looking at the dark world for which God died. I don't want to live in a warped relationship with God where I never feel worthy enough to be loved. I want to rest in a permanent significance and blaze boldly into the darkness. And I want to do it the moon way.

As God has brought me on my own moon journey, I've realized just how fully our generation, including the church, is saturated in the world's vocabulary and version of significance. In fact, in the church, our very desperation to change the world or matter for God's kingdom leaves us especially susceptible to the enemy's lies. We want to measure the impact we're making, count how many lives we've changed, and determine our importance or God's pleasure with us based on our calculations.

But God's kingdom operates outside of the world's rules. God designed us for His pleasure and intended that we would work alongside Him to accomplish His plan. He doesn't measure success or significance the way we do. So we have to spend more time getting to know Him and His heart in order to find the rest and joy of a moon. And getting closer to the heart of God is really what this moon journey is about.

I began to identify lies of the world (which I refer to as "star lies") and the truths of God ("moon truths") that counteract those lies. Each moon truth frees us to live more abundantly and joyfully in God's kingdom. More exciting still, as we fully embrace our own worth and purpose in the presence of God's light, we're free to light up the world around us in a profound way. As we become more like the moon, we are liberated to love others for love's sake, knowing God's love for us is permanent and complete.

As you journey through this book, you'll encounter three sections that roughly correspond to the subtitle of the book. Chapters 1-3 help you "know your worth." They identify our human desire to matter, the star lies we're following, and the truth about how God sees us. Chapters 4-8 teach us to "reflect God." They help us understand God's version of shining and the pitfalls that can keep us from shining His way. They ground us in God's design for us to shine in community and reflect Him together as His body. Chapters 9 and 10 focus on how to "light up your generation." They compel us to live out God's purpose in our time and place, and to understand that Christ is our ultimate goal. Only in Him do we find worth beyond the grave.

Each chapter ends with a "Moon University" section. Here you will discover a "Star Lie" and "Moon Truth" for each chapter, as well as study questions to go through on your own or in a small group setting. By the time you finish the book, you will have graduated "Moon University," having learned to see your worth and purpose as a moon. In graduating from the book, my hope is that you'll feel equipped to turn around and help others know their value and identity in God as well.

Even though our struggle against the world's lies will continue, my prayer is that the moon becomes a simple symbol of God's truth. I pray that every time you see the moon you would be reminded again that you are beyond loved, intrinsically valuable, and created to reflect God extravagantly in your generation. I'm so excited to walk on this journey together. May you find joy, peace, and freedom in these lessons on "How to Be a Moon."

CARRYE BURR

# 1
# SHINING: OUR QUEST TO MATTER

"'I, even I, am the Lord,
    and apart from me there is no savior.
I have revealed and saved and proclaimed—
    I, and not some foreign god among you.
You are my witnesses,' declares the Lord, 'that I am God.'"
   **-Isaiah 43:11-12**

"Blessed are those who have learned to acclaim you, who walk in the light of your presence, Lord."
   **-Psalm 89:15**

## MY STAR-TO-MOON STORY

People like to say that everyone is special, as though we were all born into some platinum club with gold membership cards. It's nice to have an imaginary flashy card that says I'm unique, but it doesn't seem to be accepted very many places (much like my Starbucks reward card). I couldn't enroll in college based solely on my individuality. Employees never hired me based on the fact that there's no one quite like me in the rest of the world. And I can be generically special all I want, but that credential isn't quite enough to convince my seven year old that he should listen to me.

The reality is, I don't always feel special, needed, or worthy. Instead, my world often feels like an ongoing series of auditions to see if I'm "enough" for the parts I want to play in my life. I daily audition for the part of "likeable" on Facebook or with friends. I audition for the role of "competent mom" whenever I take my kids to any public place. With my husband, I might be trying out for the part of "attractive" or "organized,"

5

and even with God I sometimes feel like I'm trying to earn the part of "good and faithful." I'm hoping someone will look at the application of my life and check off a little box that says I'm making a difference and I matter.

Then there are the literal auditions in my life. I decided early in my childhood that sports were better suited to people who actually like physical activity. (I also recall getting pummeled in the nose by a football during a family game. That didn't help.) Instead, I focused my energy on theater and music. As a kid, I joined church Christmas pageants and drama classes and eventually auditioned for high school theater productions. In addition to theater parts, I pounced at any chance to get a singing role.

Singing has always been like an invisible best friend that goes with me everywhere. As a mom I invent silly songs for my kids and alter the lyrics to real songs in an attempt to narrate my life. (Usually late at night.) You have to be careful not to say anything around me that reminds me of pop lyrics, because you will trigger an involuntary song explosion. If you're not quite as musically awkward as I am, just picture that obnoxious musical person in your own life. I'm sure you have one.

I grew up in a musically gifted family, the kind that hauls guitars and cellos on family vacations, and belts out "Happy Birthday" in three part harmony. My mom taught me to harmonize when I was a kid, in part because the melodies to most songs were too high for me to sing. My attempts at soprano notes were about as painful as listening to a room full of third graders playing recorder. But harmony made me feel like I had something to offer, as though perhaps I really were special.

As I matured into my unique voice, I also stumbled into insecurity. Long before *American Idol*, I discovered singing was a spectator sport where others could cast their votes of approval or otherwise. It was just one more avenue for people to check off that box to determine my significance. As a pastor's kid, my church provided plenty of opportunities to showcase my talent. In addition to the thrill of doing what I loved, I soon found myself addicted to the compliments and praise that came with performing publicly.

So often the things we love to do are also the places where we most seek to define ourselves through the approval of others. The gifts and passions that intrinsically give our souls satisfaction quickly turn into an insatiable quest to know and prove that we matter.

So how did that quest play out for me? Well, when I wasn't crooning just for myself in the shower, I sought out ways to perform for others. I eked out a solo in my elementary school concert, harmonized in youth group band, and tried out for high school choir.

I believed that I had a good voice, but it wasn't until someone actually picked me out and invited me to sing that I really felt worthy. I became wrapped in the lie that my value could only be as great as the role someone else allowed me to have: as a mother, as a writer, as a leader, and certainly as a singer.

As an adult, of all the singing roles I could hope to be granted, the holy grail of vocal worth was to be picked for...wait for it...the church worship team. For a church-grown girl, a spot on the worship team was a double win; it satisfied my desire to sing for others, while also allowing me to use my voice as a gift of worship to God. I desperately wanted my life and gifts to matter to God and be used for His kingdom. But, I would quickly learn, it was all too easy to get my gifts and ministry FOR God tangled up with my identity IN Him.

At first, fear of making a mistake (and losing my significance) made me timid. I never attempted any high notes, and left an awkward space between me and the microphone, as though it were my first high school dance partner. The sound guys told me to "eat" the mic- I'd rather exchange pleasantries from a distance. I didn't want to put too much of myself out there, only to fail and have my newfound role ripped away.

But eventually the awkward evolved into a comfortable rhythm. As nervous as I was to screw up a song (which I did plenty, by the way), I relished being on stage, belting out my harmonies, and savoring the occasional solos.

Don't get me wrong, I wasn't purely glory seeking; I love worshipping God through singing. There's something about the way I feel His presence while creating music that I can't duplicate elsewhere. God gives us gifts and passions to enjoy with Him and we shouldn't feel guilty for relishing the unique places for which He has designed us.

But we have to be careful that our passions don't become the measuring stick of our value. As my role on the worship team became dangerously wrapped up in my identity, pride and striving crept in unannounced. I started craving more influence, more opportunities, and more applause.

I didn't just want to sing anymore; I wanted to use up my full vocal potential and be really useful. I bought into the lie that the higher up the ladder I moved, the more I'd matter. For people. For God. I'd have an indisputable rock on which to stake my significance and kingdom impact.

But it didn't really matter what people in general thought- I felt that the worship leader was the one who held the keys to unlock my potential publicly. I thought if he would just give me the chance to have a few good solos and really break out, he'd see.

A side-effect to believing that someone else sets the limit of our worth is that we tend to walk as victims of others, blaming them when we don't feel like we're enough. Maybe we stop enjoying our gift unless we can control how we use it. Or we compare ourselves to those who are living our dream role and think, "*If I only had the opportunities they have. If only someone would give me a turn.*"

I had my own victim excuses and envious wish-list. See, I wasn't on the rotation as frequently as the other worship team girls, and I felt doomed to lead the lackluster songs, locked in by a lethal combination of my low vocal range, song key selection, and an inability to harness any kind of spontaneous ethereal sound. My soprano background "oohs" would be better suited to distract a dog than to compliment "I Can Only Imagine." *"If I could just trade this voice in for a higher one, God. Please and thank you."*

Looking back, I recognize that season for the amazing opportunity it was to worship with and serve others. In fact, there may have been others who wished they had even half of my opportunities to sing on stage. But at the time, I was so focused on my limits I didn't see my liberty. So when I didn't feel like I was getting optimal accommodation of my gift, I decided I'd just have to look somewhere else to fulfill that dream.

Sometimes when we don't feel appreciated by the "audition panel" in front of us, we simply trade one judge in for another by seeking out new people to define our worth. But whenever we're looking for someone else to affirm and promote our value, we'll find it's a never-ending, soul-wearying battle.

But that's a lesson I had to learn the hard way, so I took matters into my own flawed hands. I'd find someone who would appreciate my blaze of potential. My plan was to audition for a musical in a local theater group. They were putting up *Little Shop of Horrors*, and I just knew I could run with that low, soulful part of Ronette, one of the backup trio girls. Just maybe there was a part for me. Just maybe I'd be chosen (valuable, needed, significant).

Cue yet another audition: I panic-waited outside the audition room, brushing shoulders with other girls who seemed far more talented than I was. My only hope was to somehow play my unique card and pray it worked this time. They could have all the impossibly high vocal parts, even the lead role, but not the one obvious role meant for me. *"Dear God, let them all be sopranos...or be smitten with sudden onset of severe laryngitis."*

Once inside the judgment, er, audition room, I was an awkward mess, like a gazelle pretending to be a cheetah to avoid being eaten. It wasn't pretty. The pianist didn't initially recognize my Broadway song, "Holding Out For a Hero," which I'd painstakingly picked as one of the few audition songs that matched my weird range. I foolishly planted myself in the corner by the piano so I could follow the music, instead of standing in a more professional place like, say, maybe *in front of* the audition panel. I vaguely recall stress-reading a character's line from the script and afterwards replaying all the ways I could have done it better.

By the time I left I was definitely brighter, if we're referring to my hyper-active flushed cheeks. (You don't want to take me on in a blushing competition!) I imagine I needed a deodorant reapplication as well, but there was absolutely nothing glorious in my prove-my-worth-to-the-world audition. So much for trying hard and believing in myself and all that jazz.

Ultimately, they called me back and let me down easy: even though I wasn't selected for a main role, would I like to join the show as an ensemble chorus member? The familiar disappointment in my core kicked in; maybe I was forever fated to be the glory-squashed victim of people who couldn't see my potential. God wasted a gift on me, clearly, because none of the people He created could see it.

Or maybe...what if...? There was another gnawing voice as well, one that I was scared to even admit: perhaps I wasn't as brilliant or valuable as I'd hoped. Maybe the people I'd auditioned for weren't wrong after all, and I simply wasn't as useful as I'd believed.

Maybe you've fallen into this pit right along with me, believing that God may give us gifts, but the world ultimately gets to decide whether our gifts are enough. So you feel crushed when your boss passes over you for that promotion, or you just missed the cut for the varsity sports team, or that writing piece you labored over isn't selected for publication. Our reaction to rejection is to constantly look around, hoping that someone somewhere will give us a higher appraisal on our worth.

When I got the rejection call that I didn't make the audition cut, I didn't rejoice that at least I was still fearfully and wonderfully made. I didn't wink at God and enjoy the fact that other talented people did get lead roles. Nope. I moved on to Carrye's plan-B.

In that moment I figured I'd accept the chorus role and scrape the glory off the sides of the mixing bowl at least. I pushed my thoughts of inadequacy aside, hoping to grab at any potential sparkle left to be salvaged in this rapidly unraveling story. Besides, since I lived my life like an improv musical anyway, how could this be anything other than fun?

I was so wrong. (Cue some dissonant chords!) Out of practice, the chorus sheet music was about as useful to me as a Zamboni in my living room, and the practices were painfully disorganized. I'm 98.3% sure I got off on the wrong foot with the director, and that was before I was given the non-speaking role of a pimp in the "Skid-Row" song. The directing team took pity on my painfully awkward attempt at pimpness (it wasn't really in my "good Christian girl" repertoire), and they quickly transitioned me into a sort of depressing nun. Talk about a 180.

Feelings of foolishness and disappointment set in. If I wasn't a lead then I was expendable- a placeholder. My gift was just the same as lots of people's gifts, apparently. Didn't that mean that my gift was less valuable-that I was less valuable? I began to resent rehearsals for taking my limited free time away from my small children without offering me anything shiny in return. It wasn't until I humbled myself enough to at least help the crew backstage that I accidentally enjoyed myself.

I see now how selfish I'd become (I wish I could speed up the process of hindsight.) I was so concerned with amplifying my own worth, I failed to see how my piece was meant to lift up the whole cast. Instead, I found it easier to view the cast as competition- little glory magnets that were stronger and more powerful than I was.

Come show time, I was still so focused on myself that I didn't feel like inviting anyone. I'd rather hide a little deeper in my borrowed nun costume and close my eyes till I could just be done with the apparent fiasco. I enjoyed moving props backstage where at least I felt needed, and ultimately I found the theater group to be full of wonderful people.

But my experiment had failed: one more audition panel told me my voice wasn't quite good enough for me to really be important...like a star.

## THE WORLD'S "STAR" LIE

In my quest to matter, I'd taken the gifts God had given me but neglected to rest in His purpose for me. I believed the world's American-dream, star-dazzling lie that I had to leverage what God gave me and prove to Him and everyone around me that I was worth seeing, worth belonging. I thought I needed to do more and be more.

I wish I could say that I only struggle to know my worth when it comes to singing. But I've found myself craving shine in most areas of my life: writing, parenting, cooking, friendships, speaking, social media, ministry, and beyond.

Apparently, I wasn't just getting cozy with the world's star lies; I was full-on dating them. Most of us have subtly bought into a world that values bright things- not just shiny things, "shinier-than" things. We learn quickly that our brightness is largely based on our performance or appearance compared to others- whether we stand out in the crowd in the right ways. Are we cutting edge or outdated? Are we just a number or uniquely useful? Are we able to measure what we can offer the world?

Certainly by high school, when we start filling out college and job applications, we find that a degree isn't sufficient; we need academic clubs, extracurricular activities or over-the-top volunteer work to be noticed. We need to prove to the powers that be (who are always changing, by the way) that we are valuable. I'm breaking out in stress hives just thinking about it.

If you're a human with a pulse you've probably had a moment in your life when you didn't feel like you measured up. Whether we're chasing academic dreams, business success, perfect family, or health goals, we can feel like our worth won't be secure until we perfect or accomplish that next thing. There's always someone else to prove ourselves to or something else that we think will finally supply our value.

This transfers to our spiritual lives as well. We truly desire to love God by serving the world. We want to be a bright light in all the right ways because God says we're meant to shine like stars. But we use the world's version of success to determine our kingdom productivity.

We fear we don't matter to the body of Christ or to God Himself if we're not racking up spiritual converts, reaching millions for Christ on Twitter, or if we don't seem to be good enough to join the "important" church ministries. Without discernment, church culture doesn't always remove us from the world's lies; sometimes it just twists them into lies that sound spiritual.

Seasons of success pose a new problem. Maybe you get into that prestigious college with a full scholarship; maybe you land a dream job or your fantasy family or, be still my soul, a coveted spot on the church worship team. There's nothing wrong with that! But if those bright places of success start to define us, we'll find our gifts can enslave us to pride or to the pressure of living up to everyone's expectations.

Maybe you're not a spotlight person like me. Maybe you've never felt your light slipping out of reach from the inside of a cheap nun costume. But I'm convinced that our desire to be bright isn't just related to whether we crave a stage or not.

Our desire to be bright is really our desire to matter. Because the world says bright things matter.

My quest to find value in singing is the same quest of everyone who has ever felt the need to prove their own value or to measure their purpose. It's our heart's longing to know that everything we do, from parenting to painting a bedroom, has meaning. We may not even recognize how much this quest controls our thinking until we ask ourselves some difficult, blunt questions. Try these on for size:

- Do you feel like you are enough (sufficiently valuable) if you never accomplish anything more in your life?
- Are you constantly comparing yourself to other people wondering if you measure up?
- Would you feel less valuable if you suddenly lost a position, role or relationship?
- Do you find that your emotions rise and fall with every compliment or criticism?
- Is your desire to serve others sometimes eclipsed by your desire to matter to others?
- Can you think of specific people from whom you are striving to get approval?
- Are you afraid you'll shine too much or too little to make God happy?

The way we answer those questions says a lot about who we are believing. If you've struggled to find your worth according to the world, let me tell you right now that the world is a liar. The world is Enemy territory and that means loving the world and its value system will inevitably rob us of the value God has freely given us. But in God's presence, we find our true identity and lead others to know theirs as well.

Maybe we weren't made to be stars at all.

## JOHN THE BAPTIST WAS A MOON

John the Baptist is one of my favorite people from the Bible, and not because I have a weakness for guys with a lot of hair. I love John because he was willing to say out loud what most of us are afraid to whisper under our breath.

He was so confident of his purpose and God's truth that he challenged everyone he encountered to give up their life of sin and turn to God, and he denounced prominent religious authorities without batting an eyelash. Yet when John was locked in prison, he wasn't afraid to admit his doubts about Jesus either, wondering why Jesus was healing and saving everyone except him.

Despite John's human doubts and shortcomings, Jesus Himself gave John the greatest recommendation letter I've ever heard: "...among those born of women there has not risen anyone greater than John the Baptist..." (Matthew 11:11) Now THAT'S what I'd like on my resume. "Surpassed by 0." And to hear that spoken to me by God? I mean, there's not an audition that would matter more to me than God's "well done."

I'd be tempted to say we're all competing for a silver medal, standing just a little lower than John on a podium near the streets of gold. But Jesus followed up his glowing recommendation of John with a seeming contradiction: "...yet whoever is least in the kingdom of heaven is greater than he." (verse 11)

What on earth did Jesus mean? If John is the greatest, he's the star! He's the pick of the litter, the cream of the crop, and every other cliché you can think of for "best." How could the least person in God's kingdom be greater than John? But Jesus was trying to rip open the veil between His kingdom and the world. He was trying to show us that the way to matter is not what we've been told.

John already knew the answer to being great in God's kingdom. He was raised on the fringes of society, in the wilderness, paying little attention to the world's standards of eating habits (he ate locusts and honey) much less its rules about our souls. John had a single focus: to prepare the world for the coming of Jesus.

In anticipation of Jesus, John had begun to baptize people as a symbol of repentance from sin. Despite his unconventional life and brusque conversation, John had gained a group of loyal followers, and people were seeking him out to be baptized. He was starting to look like a bright star of influence in the making.

But suddenly, Jesus showed up on the scene, and people gravitated towards Him instead of John. In fact, with all the attention shifting to Jesus, it looked like John might soon be out of people to baptize at all. Afraid that he was losing the edge on his fame and influence, John's followers "...came to John and said to him, 'Rabbi, that man who was with you on the other side of the Jordan—the one you testified about—look, he is baptizing, and everyone is going to him.'" (John 3:26)

John's disciples didn't have a clue. They saw Jesus as a jerk who was ruining all of John's hard-earned fight in the religious popularity contest. I mean, all that bug eating couldn't have been for nothing. He'd put in his time- didn't he deserve to move up the ladder instead of down?

Whenever I'm mad about something, I don't want to talk to someone who will remain calm and rational. I want to talk to someone who will hear me vent, be mad with me, and help me eat my feelings. But when John's friends tried to get him fired up, he was irritatingly calm.

John assuaged his agitated followers by reminding them that "'A person can receive only what is given them from heaven. You yourselves can testify that I said, 'I am not the Messiah but am sent ahead of him.' The bride belongs to the bridegroom. The friend who attends the bridegroom waits and listens for him, and is full of joy when he hears the bridegroom's voice. That joy is mine, and it is now complete. He must become greater; I must become less.'" (John 3:27-30)

John knew that his disciples' fear came from the world's lies. They had come to view John's ministry as a symbol of personal success, when in fact his ministry was given to him by God. It was all grace. John breathed the rules of a different kingdom, one that Jesus' life and death would usher in like never before. John was content to simply belong to Jesus and listen for His voice. John didn't need an audition panel to tell him his worth. He didn't need more followers- in fact, he found more joy in chasing less.

John understood that his mission was simply to be "...a witness to testify concerning that light, so that through him all might believe. He himself was not the light; he came only as a witness to the light." (John 1:7-8)

Jesus was the Light. Jesus was the Star...the Sun. John didn't need to be great by increasing his platform, and becoming the brightest light. That role is permanently taken. He simply wanted to bear witness to the brightest Light, just as the moon bears witness to the sun.

The Psalmist calls the moon, "the faithful witness in the sky" (Psalm 89:37) and there was no more faithful witness to Jesus than John. He was a powerful moon, more concerned with reflecting Jesus than elevating himself. His words to his disciples convict me too; I didn't realize that in all my striving for more significance, I was trying to take the star position of glory that belongs to God alone. If Jesus came to sing on my worship team, I might have asked him to please move out of the way because He was ruining my opportunity to matter for Him.

I didn't know that in my pursuit of worth, I was running full speed in the wrong direction. I was irritated and joyless, pointing to myself instead of God. Yet Jesus whispers in love to me...to you...that whenever we're ready to stoop low and give up our lives to serve, we can be just as bright as John- who is just as bright as the One he's reflecting.

Full joy and rest can be ours when we stop clawing and gasping for worth, and learn to find more by giving up. We can allow God to renew us through the countercultural truths of His kingdom, and to reflect His heart and character powerfully in our lives. Living as a moon isn't just a cute idea, it's our calling. Our entire lives were designed to bear witness to God. That's what this book is about. Are you in?

You've just signed up for a journey away from empty, self-made brightness into a more glorious light than you could ever have believed. You've joined a movement of people ready to reclaim their identity and blaze brightly as a witness to God. You've lived the unsatisfying exhaustion of striving for man-made "star" value, and you're ready to rest as a reflector instead.

Stars are responsible for creating their own light, so if we take our cue from them we wind up weary and insecure, striving and competing. But the moon has a different brand of shining to teach us. Our moon does shine like a star- like the stunning sun that it reflects. But it doesn't have to break a sweat trying to reach new levels of glowing, and neither do we. If Jesus is our Sun, we can rest in His presence, discover our precious value, and reflect His glorious light to a generation waiting for hope.

It's time to be honest about our quest to matter and allow God to renew our minds to be like Him. It's time to learn how to be a moon.

## MOON UNIVERSITY
### Lesson One

**Star Lie #1**: Our mission is to do more and be more to prove our worth.

**Moon Truth #1**: Our mission is to surrender so more of God is reflected.

Question 1: Do you have an "audition" story from your own life- a memorable moment when you were trying to find validation of your worth?

Question 2: Who is your current "audition panel"- the person or people in your life that you're waiting on to approve your worth or validate your gift?

Question 3: Where in your life have you succeeded in feeling "shiny" (through accomplishments, praise, or abilities)? Do you feel like you have to maintain that worth?

Question 4: After reading the list of questions about your worth on page seven, did you find that any resonated with you more than others?

Would you add any questions to that list from your own life experience?

Question 5: What sticks out to you from the story of John the Baptist? What does it mean in your own life to be less so God can be more?

Question 6: What are you hoping to find on your journey to learn "how to be a moon"?

2

# SHINING DOESN'T DEFINE OUR WORTH

"And I pray that you, being rooted and established in love, may have power, together with all the Lord's holy people, to grasp how wide and long and high and deep is the love of Christ, and to know this love that surpasses knowledge—that you may be filled to the measure of all the fullness of God."
   **-Ephesians 3:17-19**

### FINDING WORTH BEYOND OUR GLOW

As we begin our journey to live like a moon, we need to understand an important truth: we were created to shine, but shining doesn't create our worth. In fact, one of the greatest barriers to experiencing the full life God intends for us is believing that our significance is directly tied into our roles and actions. To show you what I mean, I'll have to share a super high-tech moon experiment.

Once upon a time I was in the middle of a very experimental homeschool season, chasing an imaginary dream of continuously giggling children, educational fun, and cuddling on the couch with books. We had some good days. Ahem. Sure.

But it turns out homeschooling turned me into monster mom (momster?) far too frequently. I have faint blurry memories that involve an overlooked toddler, academic rebellion, enough encyclopedias to start a bonfire, and field trips gone awry. Apparently two year olds see no difference between the furniture they climb on at home, and the brittle, historically irreplaceable furnishings of the Harriet Beecher Stowe house. Suffice it to say, our homeschool spree only lasted a year and a half.

On this particular day, we were experiencing a rare and magical moment of schooling bliss as we attempted another homemade science experiment. We were studying the solar system, and a glossy apple was supposed to be the moon. Ok. I lied about this being high-tech. Roll with me here.

I stabbed the apple with a pencil and we brought the skewered fruit into our darkened guest room. The kids took turns being the "Earth," slowly spinning in place while holding the apple. Meanwhile, one of us held a flashlight that represented the sun. As the kids rotated, they could see from the Earth's perspective how the moon appears to change shape in each moon-phase. We were doing well till one of the boys snacked on the moon.

Now, call me Captain Obvious, but that apple didn't glow on its own. I wouldn't have let my son eat it if it did, although after three kids I have fewer scruples about what constitutes "inedible." But without a flashlight present, my kids would've just been twirling an apple on a stick in the dark. Awkward.

We'd all be freaked out if an apple suddenly glowed on its own, but we forget sometimes that the moon isn't naturally bright either. We regularly watch it light up our sky and, if you're a moon fanatic like me, you miss it when it isn't visible. Yet the moon isn't a light at all, which poses a major problem if our light is what gives us value.

I selfishly wanted the goal of moon-training to be about harnessing God's light so that...wait for it...I could matter more. Maybe we could all just follow a few simple steps to being the best reflector we can be, angling ourselves just right, and polishing up our moon dust a little for optimal glow. Then we could take a little credit for our shine and take our worth back into our own hands.

But God has been slowly, even painfully, teaching me that I've got to let go of everything I thought I knew about shining in order to find Him. He's stretched my ego-filled, puffed up view of human glory, like a balloon that popped in my face and left me with nothing. And nothing is absolutely terrifying because I can't make anything out of it. Yet nothing is precisely what God works best with.

The first step to being a God-glorifying moon is to fully take in our moon-dust-dullness. As a moon, you can't create light or even a slight glittery shimmer. Every one of us falls short of God's glory and all our attempts to shine apart from God are futile. (Maybe not my finest pep talk.)

On a related note, you are immensely more valuable than you currently believe. In God's kingdom, our worth is never dependent on who WE are but on who GOD is and the way He sees us. It turns out, immeasurable worth isn't a matter of what we can offer or accomplish- it's simply our birthright. You read that right. You don't have to do a thing to matter.

In our human attempts to shine, we're actually running ourselves ragged seeking a self-worth that God has already given us. Our frenzied desire to find purpose makes us live like multitasking, crazy people, insecure and distracted from God's heart.

So how do we stop the crazy and become transformed to God's value system so we can shine powerfully and securely in our generation?

I'm going to let you in on a two-part secret that you probably already know. But we have a tendency to believe things in our minds and live like we believe the opposite. (Just like I believe that bees aren't intentionally out to get me, but I often act like they've formed a highly-organized, mass conspiracy to take me down.) What I'm about to say is so simple that we easily miss the full implications it has on our lives.

**Painfully obvious truth #1**: If we're all created, our Maker assigns our value.

When someone creates something, be it a painting or a clay pot, the designer assigns value to that creation. Let's say my three year old son squishes a little ball of clay between his dimpled fingers and proudly proclaims that he's created "Daddy." The clay lump would have no retail value- it probably isn't even recognizable as a human. (He's still at the anatomically illogical stage where arms are attached to heads.)

But even if no one else would ever pay a cent for it, that clay matters to my son. He envisioned a reality for that clay and formed it on purpose. He's proud to call that misshapen "Dad" his own, his art, his delight even.

God is like my three year old son in His joy over us. Psalm 139 says God made us "fearfully and wonderfully" (vs 14) and He's "familiar with all [our] ways" (vs 3). In fact the psalmist goes on to say, "Your eyes saw my unformed body; all the days ordained for me were written in your book before one of them came to be. How precious to me are your thoughts, God!" (vs 16-17)

God is intimately acquainted with exactly who you are and cared enough to take note of each minute of your life before you took your first breath. Which brings me to the next point:

**Painfully obvious truth #2**: Our Creator assigns us top value.

If I had a nickel for every time I heard the phrase "Jesus loves you" as a child, I could afford my own personal cafe by now. But hearing isn't believing, and there are many who struggle deeply to believe this for themselves. It's like an epidemic; I know because I'm infected.

I always found it easy to believe that God loved others but much harder to believe that He specifically loved me, let alone liked me. Somehow it sounds almost sacrilegious or selfish to consider God loving me individually, because who am I to be loved by Perfection?

I know that as creations, we're like lumps of clay: we don't have anything to offer God that wasn't given to us by Him first. I bristle at that because I want to be able to do something to be more lovable and valuable. We don't have any independent shine to bargain with here, all we have is grace. So if we're dependent on God for everything, the question becomes: How does our Creator value us as-is? What would He pay for us when we have nothing original to give back?

I think you've heard the story- our Creator designed us in His image. Unlike my son's ambiguous clay creation, God made us intentionally after Himself, which is our first clue about the extent of the worth He gave us.

Micah 6:8 says that God's desire for us is "To act justly and to love mercy and to walk humbly with your God, to be like Him." He wants us to walk with Him in relationship! We make time for the things we value, and God had nothing but time to give us since He made us for His own enjoyment. He's always cared more about our presence with Him than our productivity for Him.

God never devalued us- in fact, our first problem was that we began to devalue Him. I could rail against Eve all I want, but we're all prone to the disease of minimizing God. Eve's first problem, before even taking a bite of that fabled fruit, was to give more weight to what someone else said over what her Creator said. Does that sound familiar? We ignored the only One who can assign worth, and we've been grasping for significance ever since.

But God didn't stop actively valuing us after creation. He saw us, beautiful and needy, using borrowed breath and limbs on loan to scrounge up worth and fill our souls. And He loved us.

We had rejected Him, ignored His role as Glory-giver, and tainted the world He intended as paradise. But He knew He could restore what we broke, realign our wandering hearts to His own, and defeat the curse that ever separated us from knowing our value in Him.

So He came and allowed Himself to become the Created-Creator, Master Potter-turned-into-clay. He chose to become frail and small, to give up every rightful advantage, and walk side by side with His clay-gone-astray. He looked with deep love at us stubborn, fearful, lost ones. We thought we were like damaged merchandise that customers will only buy on clearance. But God determined that we, in all our scratch-and-dent form, were worth no less than His very life. That's more than full price, by the way.

So on the cross that we've often sterilized into symbolism, Jesus assigned our value and backed it with His blood: We. Are. Priceless. He died for us "while we were still sinners," (Romans 5:8) proving there was nothing He wouldn't pay for us, and not just the ones with no chipped teeth or splotchy morals. Our Creator flipping loves not just the world, but specifically me, and specifically you. No matter your background, personality, orientation, ethnicity, hair color, or gender.

Our glorious worth is pre-assigned- before we ever fix a single mistake, before we ever change another person's life for the better, before we even signed up to shine. Absolutely nothing you do can make you less valuable.

Breathe that in for a moment. We've been conditioned to think that mistakes or flaws are like grime ever-accumulating green and putrid over our worth. Every time we fail our child, act in anger, rush into a bad decision, drop the ball, or don't fit in somebody's view of normal, we can feel our worth draining steadily. When we believe the lie that we're responsible for our value, our worth rises and plummets on a daily basis. The belief that we're in control of how much God loves us is killing us.

In that twisted mindset I get bonus lovable points for staying calm when my son throws a cup at my head while I'm driving, but I lose more points for screaming like a mad-woman when the children turn bedtime into a game called "101 Ways to Not Accomplish Anything." I get bonus points for finished laundry (which, let's be honest, is a myth), but I lose points for cutting down my husband when he just needs support. I get bonus points for giving up coffee for Lent, and lose points for having an uninvited lustful thought. At the end of the day I'm lucky if I'm netting zero.

You get the picture. The offensively freeing truth is that whether you lied to your mom about how you felt about her Christmas gift or literally killed someone, your worth is undiminished in God's eyes. In either scenario He created you and died for you. And He didn't come to call the perfect, but the blemished- the sinners- the sick. All of us.

If that sounds really beautiful and you're feeling a little high on emotions right now, let me bring you down a notch to the equally freeing but more humbling reality: You can't do anything to make yourself more valuable either.

See, the other side to the God-assigned-worth coin is that in Christ we've already reached our maximum worth. That's the ceiling. There simply isn't a higher level to be attained. We should be doing backflips and cartwheels over this truth, but instead we dismiss it because it doesn't jive with our works-to-worth mentality.

The funny thing is, when we're at our lowest points, overwhelmed by our inadequacy, we're bewildered by this grace of God. We're astonished at the worth He labels us with. He points to us and says *"I'd give my life for you all over again,"* and we look over our shoulder as though He's talking to someone else and say, *"Who, me?"*

But sometimes once we're coasting down what we assume is the straight and narrow, we feel like we've outgrown grace. We believe that the bonus points of our bogus righteousness actually outweigh our sins, if we'd even call them that. We'd prefer to settle into our man-made glitter and rest assured that we can prove our worth based on who we're better than.

Or we look at God's ocean of grace and say, *"Don't worry, I'll earn my keep, I'll pay you back"* as we run weary, filling measuring cups to dump in our sand buckets, thinking we can match His abundance.

And He whispers, *"Slow down, Child. You're enough because I've made you so. And so are the ones you think you've out-performed, by the way."*

This glory-grabbing lie is more sinister than the first because we believe that we can accumulate worth apart from God. We believe that God's grace is like a parent teaching their kid to ride a bike without training wheels; maybe God runs next to us just long enough to hold us up till we're steady, then backs away so we can ride off in a blaze of our own glory. We believe, in the end, we can be more without His grace.

But God's value system is an unflinching equalizer. Whether we even believe in God or not, our worth is never in question. There are no levels of grace, no tiers of significance in God's kingdom.

So what if we lived like that's actually true?

Then even if I die today, with an unfinished book, a massive stack of dirty dishes, and a dismal amount of mistakes I never made up for, I'm gloriously valuable.

Even if your greatest career achievement is minimum wage at a fast-food chain, you are just as glorious as a CEO making six figures.

If you never make the sports team, the honor-roll, that paid ministry position, the lead in a local musical- you're as glorious unpicked as you'd be if you were chosen.

If you never lose the weight, afford the name-brand jeans, carve out that six-pack, or figure out how to accurately apply tanning lotion that doesn't make you look orange- you are stunningly glorious as is.

Even if you do all the things you told yourself yesterday you'd stop doing- you aren't dented or scratched: you're still glorious because God sees you through the perfect lens of Jesus.

This is so simple, but my heart has felt lighter these last few weeks as I've allowed this truth to sink deeply into my soul like dark stain on wood. Thus, our journey to blaze brightly begins, somewhat uncomfortably, in recognizing that "bright" isn't the destination that defines our worth. The light we shine as a moon isn't about being more but reflecting more.

There's a difference. A star shines to matter. A moon shines to mirror its Maker. When we fundamentally shift from the world's value system to God's value system, we're free! If shining isn't a competition for importance, then it becomes relational, creative, dare I say...enjoyable. You were born to shine with nothing to prove.

And if God alone defines our worth, then there's one more glory-pitfall we need to visit on our path to unlearn the world's lies and shine our hearts out.

## MOON UNIVERSITY
### Lesson Two

**Star Lie #2:** We are responsible for creating and maintaining our value.

**Moon Truth #2:** God has given us top-shelf worth that will never increase or decrease.

Question 1: Is it terrifying or liberating to think that you can't create your own value?

Question 2: Have you ever wondered whether God really loves you or likes you? How do you feel knowing that God designed you intentionally and died for you as-is?

Question 3: How do you feel about the statement that nothing you do adds MORE value to your worth? Why?

Question 4: What is one area of your life where you're trying to make God happy? What would it look like for you to accept His pre-defined worth for you and just enjoy walking with Him?

# 3
# ADDRESSING AUDIENCE

"Stop trusting in mere humans,
　who have but a breath in their nostrils.
Why hold them in esteem?"
　**-Isaiah 2:22**

"The Lord your God is with you,
　the Mighty Warrior who saves.
He will take great delight in you;
　in his love he will no longer rebuke you,
　but will rejoice over you with singing."
　**-Zephaniah 3:17**

## DANCING WITH THE STAR

I wish that you and I could simply pick up our worth in God, walk away like we're a million bucks, and never look back to our old insecurity. But for most of us, even after embracing the fact that our shine doesn't give us value, we're going to have to address another tiny little obstacle to being a moon: our obsession with audience.

Even before the internet explosion of Facebook and beyond, I bought into the lie that significance was somehow tied into how many friends I had, and being witty or cool enough to keep those friends. My friends and family were the audience that gave me a feeling of value. If I was excluded, misunderstood, or unable to keep people happy, my worth dropped on a dime. My life was a daily audition.

When I hit my early teen years, groundbreaking AOL Instant Messenger gave me the faintest taste of what it felt like to be chosen or wanted in the virtual world. (Some of you may be young enough to have missed that fleeting online chat platform that ultimately faded when Myspace and Facebook came on the scene.) Mostly I'd stare at the computer screen (after waiting on my dial-up internet, of course) and feel my heart beat fast if I heard that magical "opening door" sound effect alerting me that a guy I liked came online.

Then I'd sit there racking my brain over something witty to say, and I usually wound up saying nothing at all. I did a lot of staring at virtual doors in my day. Worse than having someone not see me would be for them to see me and reject me. Maybe, like me, you played it safe, never risking too much of yourself for fear your audience (friends, co-workers, boss, parents, etc.) might not approve.

By the time my college days rolled around, my desperation for audience was growing as fast as the internet and social media options for finding said audience. From Facebook likes and follows to Pinterest repins (repinning is the sincerest form of flattery), I've slowly become addicted to finding value in my own little virtual world of audience. Maybe you've struggled with online audience as well or maybe your crowd is mostly offline.

I realized my full on obsession with audience one night when my younger brother came over to hang out. Our cozy living room beckoned us to savor deep conversation over a warm beverage. That evening, as we chatted, I parked myself at the computer thinking I could manage to simultaneously bare my soul and download my latest family pictures from my camera so I could post them on Facebook. (Because, if you haven't heard, stars matter more if they can accomplish multiple things at once.)

My camera memory card was more stubborn than my toddler, so I quickly ran into technical difficulties and couldn't upload a blessed photo. Yes, I tried the old "turn it off and back on" trick with no luck. After several minutes, by Einstein's definition, my repeated attempts to fix my camera qualified as insanity. In my increasing frustration, just shy of putting my camera in extended time-out, I said something I immediately regretted: *"If I don't put my pictures on Facebook does the moment even count?!"*

Yikes! The revealing words just schmoozed their way out. Like aftershocks of an earthquake, they shook me awake to an embarrassing reality: I'd come to believe that the things I did as a person no longer mattered without someone witnessing them publicly.

It didn't matter if I went pumpkin picking with my kids unless someone could comment on my adorably mismatched children and our overly priced pumpkins straight from the patch. My fancy outfit for an anniversary dinner may as well have been a t-shirt and jeans if it didn't end up on someone's newsfeed.

But when I type or speak out those lies in blunt form, I'm suddenly aware of the negative hamster wheel I'm running on when I chase audience.

The need for audience is one of the greatest threats to our ability to be a moon and rest in our identity as children of God. The devastating result is that we're constantly measuring the things we do through the lens of our audience of choice: social media, church congregation, significant other, extended family, corporate world and beyond.

Reality TV has only served to escalate our false views of audience. Even if you're always a step behind popular television like me, you've probably heard of the hit competition, *Dancing With the Stars*. Each week a professional dancer and learning-to-dance celebrity partner practice new routines and try to outperform other dance couples.

The judges and spectators have complete say over how praiseworthy a dance couple is. If you're likeable and have an impeccable dance routine that dwarfs someone else's, then you're as shiny as all the sequins on those dance outfits. In other words, you matter enough to make it to the next round. If not, well... the audience literally sends you home.

We're pounded like seawalls over and over again by the unrelenting surf of a culture that idolizes audience. Sadly, the idea of audience has subtly crept into the way we view God Himself, undermining our Christ-paid-for, no-strings-attached worth.

You may have heard the saying that we're supposed to live for an audience of One: God Himself. It always made sense to me because I was conditioned to believe that I needed to perform for someone. That phrase is meant to keep us from running after the approval of the lesser audience by focusing on the audience of God alone.

We get appropriately excited about waiting for His "well done" when our life is over, and we know that we're meant to praise and obey only Him. But we have to be careful not to view God through the world's vocabulary.

When I think of God as my audience, it doesn't feel like a two-way street. It still feels like I'm supposed to be doing my little performance of obedience and praise, while He sits somewhere out in the bright lights waiting to applaud or boo me. In that case, my "well done" is based on what I do, not on the fact that He's producing fruit in me as I remain in Him. Anything that suggests we have to perform for God leads us away from the idea that our worth is pre-secured in Him.

God isn't my audience, He's right on the stage with me. And this stage isn't the place for a choreographed, rehearsed script; it's more like improv theater or a spontaneous ballet where there's give and take in the moment. God defined us when He created us and called us to be His own, so we're loved regardless of what we do or fail to do. God is enthralled in creating with me and letting me move as He teaches me to mimic His own motion, watch Him work, and rest in Him. He created in love, and He continues to create in and with me. (And in and with you.)

In Matthew 11:28-30 (MSG) Jesus summarizes this dance routine:

"Are you tired? Worn out? Burned out on religion? Come to me. Get away with me and you'll recover your life. I'll show you how to take a real rest. Walk with me and work with me—watch how I do it. Learn the unforced rhythms of grace. I won't lay anything heavy or ill-fitting on you. Keep company with me and you'll learn to live freely and lightly."

It's as though Jesus is the Star Dancer and you're the apprentice. He's not training you to dance for the applause of an audience, but for His own glory and pleasure. This changes everything! Be with Him and watch Him move. Bend and dance along.

For those who aren't comfortable with the idea of tutus (certainly not my best outfit) or dancing, imagine God working with you in your element: in the sawdust of your carpentry, the colors of your art, in the grease in your auto shop or the words you pour out on your typewriter.

As you move together, He won't put anything on you that He hasn't designed you for. He's not a distant spectator, He's Emmanuel- God with you. He loves you deeply and doesn't want to rate your performance, but to breathe Himself into all that you do. He doesn't want to boo you, He wants to transform you. Every word He speaks over you calls you back to your true identity in Him. He created you, equipped you, and calls you into His design.

When we dance to be rated by God, our relationship is based on fear of failure and shame from mistakes. But when we understand that God designed us for His joy, our focus shifts from pleasing Him out of fear to pleasing Him out of love. Our dance becomes a gift to Him, not a means to pay a debt.

Yes, God is a just Judge and we'll have to answer to Him for our actions. However, the commands He lays on us aren't part of a syllabus to critique us by, but rather a law that gives us freedom.

James 2:13 reminds us that His, "mercy triumphs over judgment." He sees you as a child He created, through the lens of the cross. Because His judgment was already passed and paid for in Christ, there's no longer a deficit or demand. You're free!

You don't have to strive to make Him happy. You don't have to bite your nails after every mistake, because God gloriously folds your mistakes right into His redemptive choreography. It's not always graceful on our part, and our sin certainly lends pain and dissonance to the dance He wants for us.

But if we believe that God is right there with us, that He takes great delight in creating with us, then we'll miraculously rediscover the intrinsic joy of dancing for dancing's sake. We'll delight in moving and breathing and walking out our passions precisely because it's what we're made for and we can't hold it in. That's the power of removing God from a spectator seat.

## ALL THOSE OTHER SEATS

As we start enjoying our dance with God, we still have to address all the others seats in our theaters. (I was kind of hoping they'd disappear if we ignored them long enough.) The creations who occupy those seats do have opinions and expectations of us.

My seats are filled with four creations that I share a house with, the creations I go to church with, even the creations I interact with at school pick-up and coffee shops. Even though God is dancing right there with me, singing His love and identity over me, my gaze moves away from Him.

This is a dance after all- or a play- and it's meant to be watched. At least that's what we think. Yes, we're meant to change the world with our dance. But before we can understand how we're meant to serve the people filling our theaters, we need to realize that those people aren't there to determine our value. They've only ever had imaginary power over our worth. Our dance Partner says, "Watch my eyes, don't look away, and the world will have no hold on you."

Don't get me wrong, my extroverted soul thrives on people time. But with most encounters, I find that self-conscious is part of my default setting. Maybe you can relate to these internal thoughts: *What on earth am I wearing right now? Why did I leave the house without deodorant? Am I saying something absolutely idiotic? What must that person think of me right now? Why does everything I say come out so awkwardly?*

My children are slowly rewiring this fear of what people think in me; they're so beautifully unconcerned about the memo the world sent them about fitting into some vague mold of normal. They haven't even acknowledged the memo. This is why my four year old needs still needs to be reminded that tackle hugs make some people uncomfortable and that while playing superheroes, he shouldn't portray the Incredible Hulk as a nudist. Talk about free.

Conversely, my baby steps towards casting off inhibition in public are just sad. Spring is slowly creeping into my corner of New England and on days when the sun streams warm through the trees, I find myself running to the end of my long driveway to get the mail. I'm not sprinting to break a record, it feels more like an act of abandon to God, my arms spread, head up, even recklessly closing my eyes for a second or two. Sometimes it's the most liberated moment of my day.

But the last time I ran blind, basking in my driveway length of freedom, I opened my eyes just in time to see my next-door neighbor driving her car into the adjacent driveway. Poof! My happy feeling died on impact. That fleeting moment of whimsy left me wondering if the neighbor thought I was certifiably insane. Granted, I couldn't read her mind- she could have been thinking about what cows would look like in rain jackets. But I let her perceived thoughts control me.

Being self-conscious is really trying to fit ourselves into an imaginary idea of how we think someone else wants us to be so they don't devalue us. We get enough real life criticism to know that people don't always think well of us, and it fuels us to try to match or exceed everyone else's idea of normal.

But for me it's not just a problem of being self-conscious around others in fear that I might lose value; I'm relying on those same people to validate my life. I'm startled to find that in my quest to matter, I've forgotten Who I'm meant to matter to. I'm appalled, actually, at the number of places where I seek out the created to give me value to the exclusion of God.

I feel depressed when I make a meal that the kids would rather throw than eat. The last time I wrote a book I obsessed over the number of created people who bought or reviewed or complimented my work. Oh, and if my own sister, a creation who loves me dearly, doesn't seem to want to hang out on a particular day, my value is suddenly shaken.

Galatians 1:10 responds to this ageless struggle: "Am I now trying to win the approval of human beings, or of God? Or am I trying to please people? If I were still trying to please people, I would not be a servant of Christ." Paul reminds us that trying to please people isn't just unfortunate, it prevents us from living as a surrendered servant of Christ.

When I close my eyes and run, my heart knows Whose I am- I'm alive and valuable to God. Then I open my eyes...and I live like a moon looking to the other moons to validate it. But when a moon looks to another moon to give it glory, it's a whole lot of work for nothing.

## PHARISEES AND FAKE GLORY

Jesus had this very conversation with the Jewish leaders of His time. They wanted more than anything to be bright to others, and they were paranoid about losing out in the glory-battle with Jesus. After all, they had always been respected in other people's eyes as the indisputable authorities of morality and faith.

But much like John's disciples, when Jesus got popular, they believed He was stealing their following! He spoke with authority, and irked them by constantly calling them out on their hypocrisy. To top it off, He was constantly healing people, which they simply couldn't compete with. Much like John's disciples, they didn't understand that Jesus was the definition of glory, and their own light was wrapped up in Him. Instead, they decided he was a glory-stealer they had to take down.

They staged controversial conversations to trip Jesus up, and they twisted His goodness into defiance. In one story, they attacked Jesus for healing people on the Sabbath, which couldn't possibly coexist with God's command to rest, they said. They wrapped up their accusation by asking Him to prove the pesky little issue of where His authority came from. "*Sure you're God.*" (Heavy sarcasm) "*Ok. So...prove it.*"

Except He had proved it. Jesus knew that there was no sense in trying to convince them of His authority, knowing their hearts were far more wrapped up in their own opinions and glory than in God's.

He said, "For the works that the Father has given me to finish-- the very works that I am doing-- testify that the Father has sent me." (John 5:36) He acknowledged simply that His work was God defined, as the act of healing itself clearly pointed to the glory of the Father.

We can borrow this truth when we're tempted to give up because others are criticizing God's work in us. When our lives reflect the Father and His restorative work, we don't need any outside proof or human resume to justify who we are.

> "'And the Father who sent me has himself testified concerning me...You study the Scriptures diligently because you think that in them you have eternal life. These are the very Scriptures that testify about me, yet you refuse to come to me to have life. I do not accept glory from human beings, but I know you. I know that you do not have the love of God in your hearts. I have come in my Father's name, and you do not accept me; but if someone else comes in his own name, you will accept him. How can you believe since you accept glory from one another, but do not seek the glory that comes from the only God?'" (John 5:37-44)

Jesus didn't seek glory from other people- He didn't even accept it. He wasn't the least bit concerned for His worth; He was concerned for the hearts of the Jewish leaders who had turned their backs on the only glory that mattered. But- lightbulb moment!- when I'm operating in star shining mentality, I'm the Pharisee. I find myself not only accepting glory from others, but chasing it down ugly and obsessed like a jilted girlfriend throwing herself at her ex.

That last verse is jarring, like a gong reverberating in my head; how can I exclusively seek the glory that comes from the only God? If I'm seeking my glory (value, worth, religion) in other people, then I'm going to wind up jealous, irritable and suspicious of others who shine brightly. But far worse than that, I'm going to miss the greater joy of being with God Himself. To allow others to define our glory is to forfeit the greater glory from God.

Jesus is the most positively glorious person I can think of, and the world hated Him. Despised Him, even. (That should make us a more than a little bit uncomfortable with the world's value system.) Sure, He had a brief burst of bright-popularity, just like my glory days on the church worship team but way better. People thought He was an amazing healer or wise prophet. They thought He might even be king material. He was the people's star...until He failed to be what they wanted.

When the time came for Him to fulfill His eternal purpose, He suddenly seemed less dazzling in the world's eyes. Unlike my humiliating audition, His chance to defend Himself was before angry Jewish leaders who He'd definitely gotten off on the wrong foot with. His chance to prove Himself was not in front of a panel of judges deciding His role in a musical or his qualification for a job, but before the powerful men who could give Him life or give Him death.

When they insulted Him, He didn't forget His lines- He simply didn't feel pressed to respond. What about when they put Him on the cross and crowed vindictively that the poor, deluded "God-man" couldn't even save Himself?

He had absolutely nothing to prove to His creation...except love.

So, "when they hurled their insults at him, he did not retaliate; when he suffered, he made no threats. Instead, he entrusted himself to him who judges justly." (1 Peter 2:23)

Can you imagine if Jesus let His self-worth, His purpose, be defined by the ones He'd created? Can you imagine if He'd entrusted Himself to the rest of us instead of God? What if He told the Father, "Gee, I respect You a lot, but the people we made- well, they're calling me a failure up here on this cross. I don't think you heard me- a FAILURE. I know you know I'm God, but, ah... that's not quite cutting it. I think you can see why I need to prove them wrong."

Thank God He didn't feel the need to prove Himself to us or the story would have been so different. We're really just not cut out for defining glory. We're sickeningly wrong. We killed and despised the most glorious One who ever entered the world. Isaiah 53 says we rejected Him and "held him in low esteem."

We held our own Creator in low-esteem- we treated Him like He was worthless. If He were auditioning for our play, He didn't get the part. And yet Jesus never wavered because His glory came from God. God has given Jesus, our Creator, the Highest, most glorious position:

"God exalted him to the highest place
    and gave him the name that is above every name,

that at the name of Jesus every knee should bow,
  in heaven and on earth and under the earth,
and every tongue acknowledge that Jesus Christ is Lord,
  to the glory of God the Father. (Philippians 2:9-11)

If God defines our worth, it doesn't matter what anyone else thinks of you or if they ever approve your life. Someone will always be there to spit out accolades and criticism, as though our dance was meant for them. But instead of condemning us, the only Critic that matters is right there dancing too, helping us when we stumble, whispering His love and validation over us as we create together.

Just like *Dancing with the Stars*, Jesus is the professional Dancer who actually knows what the dance is about. He's been orchestrating the rhythm and flow since the beginning of time. Our Partner shines brighter than we can imagine. Stars need an audience to acknowledge their light.. Moons just need to know their light source.

So, if you really believe your worth is secure- if you're ready to ditch the fading light of the other moons around you, then it's time to move forward on this journey to be a moon. Now that we've determined that neither our shine nor our audience give us significance, you might be wondering, "What's the point of shining at all?" I was hoping you'd ask.

# MOON UNIVERSITY
## Lesson Three

**Star Lie #3**: We were made to perform for and be validated by an audience.

**Moon Truth #3**: God designed us for reciprocal joy as He creates with us.

Question 1: Where are you most tempted to let people around you define your worth? Why?

Question 2: Write the difference between viewing God as an audience vs. a Co-Creator. How does the distinction change the way you think about God?

Question 3: What is something God has placed on your heart that gives you great joy? How do you feel knowing He enjoys creating with you in that way?

Question 4: What is one practical thing you could do this week to pursue God's heart of freedom for you and close your eyes to the world?

Question 5: Read the following passages:

"Am I now trying to win the approval of human beings, or of God? Or am I trying to please people? If I were still trying to please people, I would not be a servant of Christ." (Galatians 1:10)

"Fear of man will prove to be a snare,
  but whoever trusts in the Lord is kept safe." (Proverbs 29:25)

How can focusing on Jesus' life give you boldness to trust in God and be a servant of Christ instead of trying to please people?

# 4
# REDEFINING SHINING

"When Jesus spoke again to the people, he said, "I am the light of the world. Whoever follows me will never walk in darkness, but will have the light of life."
**-John 8:12**

"Now the Lord is the Spirit, and where the Spirit of the Lord is, there is freedom. And we all, who with unveiled faces contemplate the Lord's glory, are being transformed into his image with ever-increasing glory, which comes from the Lord, who is the Spirit."
**-2 Corinthians 3:17-18**

## MEET YOUR LIGHT SOURCE

My morning alarm is set to go off in that mystical interlude when the sun teases with faintest light and nature is hushed in expectation- in other words, the calm before my three children wake up. You'd think I'd creep out of bed early each morning, giddy with the birds, to savor a coffee date with Jesus in the palpable peace. But, let's face it, the same children who drive my desire to find any quiet anywhere also exacerbate my obsession with sleep. I'm convinced "morning person" is an oxymoron.

Still every night, to my husband's chagrin, I set my alarm in blatant denial for that holy grail of dawn bliss. And nearly every morning, my alarm confuses me awake (what in the world is that noise at this hour?) and destroys my husband's peace not once, but for the next ninety-five minutes that I repeatedly sleep-wrestle my phone alarm into snooze. Yet whenever my man ventures a slightly critical comment about my sleep "problem", I become irrationally defensive and throw the three times that I actually did wake up right back in his 100% justified face.

On one of those anomaly mornings, I surprised even myself by waking to catch the moon set. Yes, the moon. As I sat to be with God, I marveled at the beauty of that orb, shining bright and full across the snowy horizon. Mesmerized by lunar glory, I noticed through another window that the eastern horizon was starting to change.

Soft peach color emerged, chased by vague hints of gold. It occurred to me that very shortly the moon wouldn't be the glorious attraction anymore: as the sun rose, the moon dimmed by comparison. By the time the full presence of the sun appeared in the sky, it eclipsed the glory of every other celestial body in breathtaking light.

We've been taught as former stars that we shine for ourselves as much as for anyone else. We're possessive and obsessive over the light we gather, but if we're going to live like moons we have to stop focusing on ourselves. As humble reflectors, whose light is not our own, we can't find our purpose until we focus on our Light Source.

So let's talk Light. The Bible frequently makes use of light imagery to describe God and His glory. God lives in "unapproachable light" (1 Timothy 6:16), David figuratively talks about the "brightness of his presence" (2 Samuel 22:13), and asks God to let "his face shine on us." (Psalm 4:6) Jesus says of Himself, "I am the light of the world. Whoever follows me will never walk in darkness, but will have the light of life." (John 1:12)

In Revelation 1, John describes Jesus in language so magnificent and luminescent that it's almost frightening to imagine, let alone experience. I assume this is why John promptly falls down "as though dead" (v. 17) at the sight. John has no other words to describe Jesus than that, "His face was like the sun shining in all its brilliance." (v. 16) Jesus is so bright you'd need more than a welders mask to look directly at Him.

Jesus is our Sun, our only light-source, and He's the absolute definition of Glory and Bright. He is Light. Everything He does and is shines: His being, His character, His actions, His love. Nothing can compare with Him or shine outside of Him.

God says, "I am the Lord; that is my name! I will not yield my glory to another or my praise to idols." (Isaiah 42:8) When God says He won't "yield" His glory He's not saying He won't magnify His glory through us. He's saying, "*Nothing and no one else is like me. Nothing else deserves all your attention.*"

Like moons whose reflected light pales next to light itself, we won't become brighter by staring at ourselves, but by gazing intently at the face of Jesus. Only when we've stood, naked and empty, in awe of God's indescribable glory, can we acknowledge that He is our only hope to shine at all.

Yet this isn't a depressing surrender to a petty God who wants to remind us how dull we are. He didn't create us so He could flex His glory muscles and gloat over our ineptitude. This God formed us in His image, which means He created us to be gloriously like Him. He intended all along that we would share in His brilliance, yet in His presence, in His timing.

The first reason we shine, is simply because it's a way to worship God. Think about it this way: God created you to be a reflective surface. The greatest possible gift you can give back to your Maker is to stand, arms open, surrendered to His light. In God's crazy poetic plan, He shines His glory on us which brings Him more glory.

Isaiah 43:6-7 reveals God's heart for our purpose: "Bring my sons from afar and my daughters from the ends of the earth— everyone who is called by my name, whom I created for my glory, whom I formed and made."

And 1 Peter 2:9 says, " But you are a chosen people, a royal priesthood, a holy nation, God's special possession, that you may declare the praises of him who called you out of darkness into his wonderful light."

As His treasured children, not only is our reflected light a gift of worship back to the one who made us, it's a sign of hope to those who have never encountered our Light. In the middle of the night when it seems the sun has disappeared, the moon is a witness to the world that, yes, the sun is still there, as bright as ever. In the same way, we are made to shine to bear witness to our Source to a dark world.

## MOVING FROM DARKNESS TO LIGHT

As we enter the presence of God's light, we'll find that something far deeper than superficial light transfer is happening. Ephesians 5:8-14 says,

"For you were once darkness, but now you are light in the Lord. Live as children of light  (for the fruit of the light consists in all goodness, righteousness and truth)  and find out what pleases the Lord.  Have nothing to do with the fruitless deeds of darkness, but rather expose them.  It is shameful even to mention what the disobedient do in secret. But everything exposed by the light becomes visible—and everything that is illuminated becomes a light.  This is why it is said:

'Wake up, sleeper,
  rise from the dead,
  and Christ will shine on you.'"

We used to stumble in the dark, not having truth, not knowing God. But when Christ died for us and we trusted Him, we literally became light in

Christ. His light in us bears fruit: goodness, righteousness and truth. Since God embodies all those qualities, He uses the time we spend in the light of His presence to make us more like...Himself.

Being in God's light is about being made new, made holy. Dwelling in His presence is about allowing the Holy Spirit to move in us and change us. It's about uncovering all the ways we were made in the image of our Father, and we can't be like Him unless we're watching Him and seeking to know His mind and will. There's no more glorious mission in your life than to know Jesus. Period.

And I don't just mean meeting Him once and settling for salvation. Great chat, Jesus. Thanks for saving me back there, by the way. *Winky emoticon*. No, there's so much more to knowing God than simply being saved. An intimate relationship with God goes beyond talking about the weather and commenting on the worship songs once a week in the church lobby.

I'm talking about resolute friendship that meets for coffee together to discuss real life, that is honest enough to bring up hard stuff like suffering and grief, that says, "*God, please won't you stay up late with me and whisper Your truth into my heart because I can't live a minute more without being with You.*"

When we get past the surface and stop trying to pretend with God, He shows us more of Himself. More than once I've snuck down to my basement to hide from the world (or my kids) and throw all my junk at God. Other times I've danced in my living room, feeling that, like David, I would become even more undignified than this because of God's presence. Learning to be unraveled before God isn't comfortable, but it is essential to deeper intimacy and satisfaction in God.

We see this even in our human relationships. Some of my closest friends are the ones who have seen me at my most vulnerable. They've known me to let them down, overreact, ugly cry, tell them honestly when they hurt me, and selfishly hog the most buttery popcorn from the bowl.

But in response, they've been honest with me, shared a few ugly cries of their own, and stolen my granola bars. One friend was just vulnerable enough to pour out her heart about life while I was in the middle of a stomach bug. It doesn't get much more real than that, and she's one of my closest friends to this day.

The more honest we are with Him, the more He uncovers the inconsistencies of what we're believing about Him, and reveals His true character to us. As we come to know who Jesus really is, we realize that nothing else quite satisfies us like He does. The more satisfied we are in Jesus, the more He can reflect Himself in our lives.

If you are deeply fulfilled by Jesus Himself, you'll constantly desire His presence, which is so powerful it can transform others simply through what you're reflecting. Psalms 37:4-6 says,

"Take delight in the Lord,
  and he will give you the desires of your heart.
 Commit your way to the Lord;
   trust in him and he will do this:
 He will make your righteous reward shine like the dawn,
   your vindication like the noonday sun."

Knowing God, facing fully towards Him and seeking His precious, bright face, is reward and reason enough to shine, even if there were no other benefits.  When we know Him, He fills us with His Spirit, comforts us in our weakness, and walks with us through every pain and hurt.  He reveals things to us that are beyond our comprehension, and calls us into a relationship of love like we've never experienced anywhere else.

If you don't know that peace, that love, He's waiting for you to turn towards the warmth of His light like a groom waits to see his beloved bride's face.  There's no greater love, and if you've never embraced it, by all means throw this book aside and tell God you want all of His heart, that you want Him to show you His love and hope for your life.

And if you're struggling to move towards God, I get it.  Even though moving into the light is the most freeing thing we can do, it doesn't always feel so simple.  Turning away from the things that the world focuses on apart from God is a daily battle.  On top of that, Ephesians 5:13 says that "everything exposed by the light becomes visible…"  Exposed and visible?  Um, no thank you.

I don't know about you, but I prefer not to come into the light when I'm a mess.  I don't want to be raw and naked and exposed for what I really am- so the darkness feels a lot safer.  Our Enemy twists the darkness to look like a refuge instead of the cage it really is.  And he'd prefer that we stay in darkness to hide our sins, live in shame, and walk in bondage to his destruction.

But God says, *"Come into my light! It may sting at first as you realize the depth of your need for me, but the light isn't your enemy! My light is going to make you new. My light is going to give you life. Yes, Child, and when you enter my light you become a powerful weapon against the very enemy that once held you down- you become a light that shines to lead others out of the void and death."*

This is one of the most stunning images in the Bible: everything that is illuminated becomes a light that shines back into the darkness.  That's the definition of redemption.  That's a reason to risk walking into the light though we're afraid.  Because this is exactly what we crave- to be a spark, a light to start revival in our generation.  Though we've often tangled our own glory up in our need to shine, deep down our hearts long to be used by God to break chains and lift others out of darkness.

But we have to be awake first! We have to wake up from the stupor of the world's version of glory. We have to wake up from the mindless and empty pleasures that become our gods and blur our vision of God's heart. These things can be invisible chains over our own souls, keeping us from being free enough to free others. We can't proclaim God's power until we've lived it and believe it in our own lives.

We have to drink some spiritual coffee and come alive to the mind-boggling reality that the same power that God used to resurrect Christ is available within us as His Children of the light. The world desperately needs His resurrection power, so we need to be awake and gloriously alive in His light.

## THE TRUTH ABOUT MOON PHASES

You've probably noticed by now that our journey to shine is completely dependent on us remaining in Christ. Period. Jesus says that He's like a vine and we're like His branches; without Him and outside of His work in us, we can do nothing (John 15:5). But Matthew 5:16 also says, "...let your light shine before men that they may see your good deeds and glorify your father in heaven." As we come awake to God's purpose and walk into His light, we have to battle one more sneaky star lie.

Though our goal is to be in the presence of Jesus, we quickly start to believe the world's lie that it isn't how much light we're reflecting that matters; it's how much of our light the world can see. Instead of looking at Jesus to define us, we start to assume that our impact for Christ is directly related to our increased influence on the world.

Some of us believe that early in our walk with God, we're a "crescent" moon, maybe just shining a baby sliver of fresh light back to the world. We may not feel very qualified to serve or lead others, but we're doing our best and loving God! As we progress in our education, experience, and knowledge of God and His truth, we feel like we naturally "wax" larger, from crescent to quarter to gibbous. As we jump into careers, seek more ministry opportunities, start sharing our faith, and influence more people, we unconsciously trade the truth of our pre-secure worth in Christ for a worth defined by our season.

We get stuck on this idea that more visible bright is better bright, if not for ourselves then for the kingdom of God. If our influence on the world is the new measure of our worth, then we won't be satisfied till we reach the glorious full moon season I love best. After all, the moon seems its very brightest at a peak full moon, and isn't our goal to shine as brightly as possible?

Unfortunately, this leads us right back to the myth of audience and the world itself. We're fine with shining in "little" ways at first, resting in what

God is doing through us. But as we move into "brighter" phases or seasons of our lives, we come to believe that our impact and worth in God's kingdom are growing as well.

If you've ever experienced a season of thriving you know what I'm talking about: suddenly you have record attendance at the ministry group you lead, you're reaching more and more of the world's vulnerable through your non-profit, your kids are rising and calling you blessed, or people are starting to come to you for advice because your blog or platform has taken off.

Maybe you've earned your dream degree, your finances have grown to allow you to make a huge difference for others, or it seems you're suddenly surrounded by opportunities to share with others the faith you have in God. Bigger and brighter, you believe you're in a full moon season of life and the world around seems brighter too, praise God!

However, if we're taking our cue from a moon we should note that the lunar phase doesn't end at full. No, after reaching its peak shine, a moon begins a period of waning, the light slowly decreasing towards the left side of the moon until no light is visible at all. This is simply a part of the natural life of the moon, and we don't panic or mourn the loss of the moon's significance as we witness its rhythmical metamorphosis.

But certainly this is one part of the moon we weren't meant to emulate, right? Wouldn't God's desire be that we're all gradually increasing in our reflective capacity? It might seem biblical that God wants the world always seeing our brightest self all the time. But as the moon is designed for seasons, God has intentionally designed us for seasons as well.

## SEASON OF UN-INFLUENCE

I didn't realize how much I'd bought into the lie of bright=influence until just before my thirtieth birthday. On the edge of three decades I felt all washed up. I had a good run, you know, but maybe that's all she wrote. Literally.

I'm a pastor's kid who grew up around ministry all the time. When my mom wasn't helping at church, she was home caring for me and my three siblings. So ministry or motherhood became my unconscious life goal. While I loved writing, I viewed it as a hobby, never as a practical career. So when it came time to graduate high school and choose a college and major, I was at a loss.

My indecision led me to pick a liberal arts degree at a community college where I achieved excellent grades but little life clarity. When I transferred to a Christian college in Pennsylvania, my indecision apparently transferred right with me. I had too many options and too few answers, so in the end I pulled the plug on college to pursue the one thing that did make sense at the time: getting married and starting a family.

Within six years of quitting college, I was married with three kids. I'm getting flashback exhaustion just reading that sentence. I realize what an amazing blessing it is to have a thriving family to call my own. My kids bring whimsy and warmth into my life that I couldn't have dreamed of, and I know that raising them will ultimately be one of the most beautiful ways that I reflect God's heart in this world.

But after several years of staying home with my children, God slowly began doing a new thing in me, birthing a dream that had sprouted like a giant flower I didn't remember planting.

I was asked to speak at my church one Sunday in December, and I remember sharing about the way God is authoring our lives. My feet didn't dare stray from an imaginary two by two square box behind the stand that held my notes, which I barely took my eyes off of for fear I'd forget an important line.

If we're talking shine on a scale of one to ten, that first public message was maybe a four- definitely still in the crescent phase. But speaking felt like being at home after a long vacation- like it had been waiting there for me all along. I didn't care if my platform was virtually non-existent; I was experiencing the joy of co-creating with my Maker. It was a season of truly enjoying God's presence simply for the joy of knowing Him.

In that God-space, I sensed Him speaking to me, asking me to write another message. I pointed out to God the itsy bitsy detail that no one I knew was approaching me to share another message. Not even my mother. But I felt sure God wanted me to write anyway, so I did. At the same time, I was also busy pouring my soul into my first book, *Gray Faith*.

Suddenly, it felt like all those doors I'd been quietly sitting in front of, not even sure if I should knock on, started opening up all at once. Our church was in the process of hiring a speaking pastor, so would I mind speaking once a month until they found someone?

*"Oh. Actually, yeah...funny story. I've already got something prepared."*

Then, an awesome group of women from my church agreed to act as my *Gray Faith* guinea pigs, and tested out my new book and study guide before I published it. My husband made me an amazing cover photo, and I figured out how to self-publish on Amazon. A week after publishing, I was on a plane to Michigan to attend a Christian conference called "Speak Up[1]" with tools for both writers and speakers, which confirmed my passion for both.

I don't have a list of people I was influencing at the time, but I felt like I might as well have been lighting up the world. Just picture me like Katniss from *The Hunger Games* as her parade costume explodes into flame. I was on fire, finally tasting the fulfillment of walking in a passion I didn't fully believe in until recently. No more crescent season for this girl!

I re-vamped my blog; I launched a Facebook author page; I hesitantly bought business cards as a writer and speaker. Could it be? Maybe I'd found something I was truly good at. Maybe I'd found some way to change the world outside of "just" motherhood. Maybe this was as good as a lead part in a musical or the worship team...possibly better. I was well on my way to being a full moon.

At least, that's what I assumed until the summer of book publishing turned into the fall when people stopped buying as many books. The fall turned into the winter when we finally hired that gifted speaking pastor (drat, couldn't he have been a little less fantastic?) and my once very necessary speaking role at church naturally dwindled. Even my role as mother shifted during that time. With the sharp cold of winter came the equally biting realization that homeschooling was simply too much for me to handle anymore.

So come January, barely hanging on to twenty-nine years old, I felt like I'd come to the end of my influence. Before that year I hadn't needed any of these platforms to feel successful. Not really. I didn't need to be a speaker or bestselling author. I knew I wasn't mother-of-the-year in any survey that mattered, but I wasn't doing the worst job ever with my kids.

But my twenty-ninth year felt like that burst of flame when you pour gasoline over the campfire and give it a spark, only to watch the extravagant flame fade as the fuel burns off. What was I left with? If I wasn't as good at selling books as I thought- If I wasn't really needed at church in the same way- If I couldn't be intensely shiny in my zone anymore, then what was I?

I was clearly fading. And I was disappointed because surely God's plan wasn't to set me on a full moon course only to let me dwindle right back to a baby crescent in His kingdom. I wondered if once again I wasn't enough.

But life isn't just one long stretch of increasing productivity. We aren't on a ski lift of influence where our greatness increases relative to our height on the slopes. Our activity and seasons ebb and flow, but the good news is that God actually intended it this way.

The author of Ecclesiastes echoes our soul's wrestle with seasons: "There is a time for everything, and a season for every activity under the heavens: a time to be born and a time to die, a time to plant and a time to uproot..." (Ecclesiastes 3:1-2)

He lists many other life events, some representing flourishing and others loss. Yet he goes on to say in verse 11 that God "has made everything beautiful in its time."

Though we desire constant fruitful seasons in our lives, God uses all seasons of our lives in their time for precisely His plans. We could never reap a harvest if we didn't go through a season of planting and waiting. If we recognize God's intentional hand in each season, we can freely believe that no season is less important or shiny than the others. No moon phase is wasted in our lives, and no season decreases our value.

## THE NEW MOON

How can we be so sure that our worth doesn't shift with our seasons? When we think about the phases of the moon we often forget another important truth: no matter how much of the moon appears illuminated from earth, the moon is technically always a full moon. In fact, even in the new moon phase, when the moon isn't visible to world at all, the moon is still out there shining. It's still fully reflecting the sun- we just can't see the full brightness from earth.

We can better appreciate our seasons when we recall that our end goal isn't shining for the world or for an audience, but reflecting as worship to God. No matter what our season of life, if we're fully facing our God, we're exactly where we should be. But we're so convinced that we need to reach new levels of influence that we stop resting in the intentional rhythms of God's seasons for us.

As a result, we're terrified of seasons where our influence seems to decline. No one wants the season where the ministry dwindles, our help is no longer needed, or circumstances force us to give up some of our activities. After seasons that feel intensely bright, we're once again nervous that if we're less needed or less visible, we matter less.

We tend to view these decreasing or new moon phases as a wilderness or waiting season to be dreaded. But those new moon phases in our lives might actually be some of the most important seasons of all.

If we look at the life of Jesus, we might be tempted to think that His most important kingdom season was His flourishing teaching ministry. He must have been brightest when He spoke to a spiritually hungry crowd of 5,000 people or gave the Sermon on the Mount. Or maybe it was when He healed people or was baptized publicly with God speaking and a dove descending on the scene. (That's better than any special-effects glory I've ever seen.)

But Jesus only launched his public ministry after a very intentional new moon wilderness phase. In fact, almost the instant after He was baptized, the Spirit lead Him into a physical wilderness to be tested by the Enemy. God had just spoken His identity over His Son: why didn't Jesus start pursuing that full moon, Light-of-the-world stuff right away?

A wilderness season provides intense pressure that changes our beliefs from flimsy words to solid ground on which we can build our lives. Much like the incredible heat and pressure required to change sedimentary rock into a stronger metamorphic rock, God can use the pain, pressure, and waiting of a wilderness season to fortify our faith in Him and prepare us for

His plans for us.

In the wilderness Jesus had to face the enemy's lies, just as we do. Only in conquering them, could He walk in the purpose God had for Him, fully facing His Father without turning to the world for validation. And ultimately, His laser focus on God lead Him straight to the cross, which seems like a rookie crescent moon decision. You don't need a life coach to tell you that death makes it harder to accomplish new tasks. Yet in his death, Jesus created rippling glory beyond that of any famous earthly king ever. He never took His eyes off God.

Are you going through a wilderness season right now? Do you feel like your season of influence has dwindled, or you're experiencing a pain that has caused you to step back from the ministry or passions you once championed? As our life and circumstances ebb and flow, so too our fruit and influence for God's kingdom may seem to rise and fall.

But no matter who you are or what you do, God wants to use each season in your life for His purposes. God may use some of your darkest seasons to make you new, more like Him, more satisfied in Him. He might use some of your quietest and physically incapable seasons to breathe His greatest power into. He longs to remind us that our influence was never the ultimate goal.

While God deeply cares for the world and desires that we are sharing His truth and love with others, He wants our hearts more than our numbers and accomplishments. He just wants you.

We're reflective worshippers and we shine because we're with God. He's ours and we're His no matter what the world sees. As everything else shifts and fades on earth, God's presence will never be taken from us. No matter what circumstances we find ourselves in, we are sufficient and significant in Christ.

# MOON UNIVERSITY
## Lesson Four

**Star Lie #4**: The goal of life is to shine; the brighter the better.

**Moon Truth #4**: The goal of life is to be in God's presence and let Him make us like Himself.

Question 1: Discuss with friends or make a list on your own of all the attributes of God you can think of. What would it look like for you to reflect those attributes (light) in your own life?

Question 2: What areas of your life make it hard for you to walk into God's light because of shame, fear, or discomfort?

What would freedom in your life look like if you surrendered those things to God?

Question 3: Have you experienced moments or seasons of delighting yourself in God? If so, what did that look like for you? What do you think holds you back from enjoying God?

Question 4: What season of life are you in right now? How does your current season make you feel about your worth?

Question 5: You're always a full moon if you're facing God; He uses each season in your life for a reason. Do you believe that? What implications does this have for your life?

# 5
# DARK AND LOW: WHERE WE SHINE BEST

"Arise, shine, for your light has come,
   and the glory of the Lord rises upon you.
 See, darkness covers the earth
   and thick darkness is over the peoples,
 but the Lord rises upon you
   and his glory appears over you."
**-Isaiah 60:1-2**

"You are the light of the world. A town built on a hill cannot be hidden."
   **-Matthew 5:14**

## GO LOW TO GLOW

Let's pretend that you grew up obsessively playing *Monopoly* and refused to play any other board games. You've spent countless hours moving a little dog character around the board, cashing in on real-estate ventures, avoiding jail and dreaming of owning Park Place. (You really need to get out more.)

One day, your friend rocks your world by teaching you about a new game, called *Chutes and Ladders*. The goal of this game is a lot different than *Monopoly*, but you find that it's surprisingly fun. So the next time your friend comes over, you ask to play *Chutes and Ladders* again.

But let's say that this time, you try to play the new game to the rules of your old favorite game, *Monopoly*. At first it's not so bad. The spinner will do just fine in place of the dice and in both games you begin by moving your character piece on the board. But by a couple moves in, you'll realize you've hit an impasse.

Instead of properties to collect, you run into slides. You can't be quite sure where the jail is, and the only money you see on the board is a picture of a child emptying his allowance to pay for a broken window. If by some miracle you make it to the end of the *Chutes and Ladders* game board using the wrong directions, you'd have to start back at the beginning because *Monopoly* has no finish line. Playing one game to the rules of another gets you nowhere.

In the same way, God's kingdom has an entirely different set of rules than the world's. If I'm not careful, I apply the world's values to God's "game" and wonder why I feel busy but going nowhere.

My moon heart wants to write for God, believing He's put wisdom in my heart to share with others. But the world is right there telling me to be a star. The world says that influential writers end up on the New York Times Best Seller list. The world decrees that only traditionally published authors matter. The world tells me I shouldn't even call myself a legitimate writer unless I'm making some solid Benjamins from my endeavor, or have a few thousand followers on Twitter. So I wind up discouraged when my God-dream can't meet those expectations.

Do you know what God says? He says there's rejoicing over one lost sheep that turns to Him. If God rejoices over the one, I'm part of the party whether I reach one or one-million. (And so are you!) Each life matters. The Bible says "whatever you do, work at it with all your heart as one serving the Lord." (Colossians 3:23) In fact, even if I'm never published at all and (horror of horrors!) no one sees my work, it still matters because it's done for God.

When I apply the world's rules to God's kingdom, I assume I'm somehow less important and helpful to God's kingdom than really popular Christian writers. I must be a spiritual lightweight compared to the Ann Voskamps and Max Lucados of the world, because- Gracious!- have you seen how many people they've reached through their books?

But God says I matter. You matter. And it has nothing to do with our productivity or apparent influence.

Our problem is that we ask God to provide our passion, then we ask the world to validate our progress. When we confuse our influence with worth, we become more focused on results than people. Yet constantly trying to validate our worth leaves little time for the people we're meant to serve.

Maybe Max and Ann aren't your icons of significance, but we all have people in our lives that we use as measures of our kingdom value. We believe God hasn't blessed or shown favor on us and our efforts unless He's giving us that larger circle of influence. We stop dancing with God and put Him back out in the audience with the rest of the world, and we're exhausted and disoriented as a result. Like playing *Chutes and Ladders* with the rules of *Monopoly*, trying to follow Jesus and shine like a star at the same time is terribly confusing.

Just take a cue from Jesus: He pretty much broke all the rules in the world's "Star Shining Handbook."

- The world says that important people should be served by others. Yet Jesus "did not come to be served, but to serve, and to give his life as a ransom for many." (Matthew 20:28)
- The world claims that success is moving from rags to riches, from janitor to CEO. But Jesus went from riches to rags: He "...did not consider equality with God something to be used to his own advantage; rather, he made himself nothing by taking the very nature of a servant, being made in human likeness." (Philippians 2:6-7)
- The world says guard your reputation because being seen with the wrong people could destroy your value. Jesus hung out with the sick, lame, tax-collectors and sinners, unafraid of being tainted by association.
- The world says success comes through promotion, but for Jesus the greatest success of all came through a cross. (Not many of us hope our boss will promote us straight to crucifixion.)
- The world says, "Go up to shine. You are shiniest around shiny people. Be followed to shine." Jesus says, "Go low to shine. You shine brightest where it's dark. Be a servant to shine."

## SERVING IS SHINING

Following Jesus will always be at odds with the world's methods of shining brighter, but change is hard. One of our first steps towards change is to take stock of the lies that we're prone to believe about what it means to shine in our unique situations.

I wish I could tell you what specific lies you're believing. But unless you're a married, stay-at-home mom of three who writes and speaks on the side (and hates coleslaw), you're probably not going to struggle against the same perceived rules of shining that I do.

It might take some digging, but you're the best person to uncover the star distractions in your own life. So what are the "rules for shining" in your world? It's important to move from generic lies of the world to the specific lies you believe in your life.

We have different rules based on the different roles and responsibilities in your life, so don't get stuck on just one. For example, as a stay-at-home mom, here are some lies I buy into about what makes me successful: a clean home, a happy husband, obedient children, and scheduling a haircut for my boys before they look like yetis.

As a speaker and author I have other rules for what makes me feel significant: increase blog readers, sell more books, line up more speaking engagements, and -for the love of doughnuts!- remember how to use punctuation correctly.

Your situations may be far different. If you have a career or ministry position, what are the rules of success for your job: awards, promotion, raise, or compliments, increased attendance or giving? If you're on a sports team, what is the rule of success there: getting a starting position, MVP award, top scorer, more fans? Reaching those markers in your life isn't wrong, but they can quickly become a trap instead of providing the security they falsely promise.

You can even take this exercise to a more personal level and ask yourself what "success" means in your individual relationships: with a boss, your in-laws, your spouse, your friends. We tend to believe that our ability to meet people's expectations of us is part of successful shining. Who do we most look to for validation and why?

When we seek validation from God, we can rest because we already know where we stand with Him. But when we seek approval from others, the rules are always changing and I'm waiting each day to see what validation others give me.

Does my husband give me shine by thanking me for doing dishes or deftly handling my son's meltdown? Does my pastor give me shininess by applauding my ministry work? Am I enjoyable enough for my sibling to give me validation by hanging out with me?

In the same way, Jesus' disciples had the tendency to believe that their shine came from whether they were given a title or honor that acknowledged their significance. Mark 10 provides an inside peek at the shine-struggle of James and John, two brothers nicknamed "sons of thunder," a clue to their big and bold personalities.

One day, the two of them were in search of some serious validation and felt the need to ask Jesus for the ultimate gold star sticker icon of importance: the chance for each of them to have a seat on His right and left side when He came into His glory.

Jesus quickly shut the conversation down. These ministry-men-in-training believed their path to shining required Jesus to give them validation through a physical place of honor. If they just got Jesus to sign off on some merit badge, they would know without a doubt that they were significant, needed, valued.

But Jesus completely upended their definition of success. He said in verses 43-44 "...whoever wants to become great among you must be your servant, and whoever wants to be first must be slave of all."

They were trying so hard to rise higher, get ahead of the other disciples, distinguish themselves as the disciple-elite. But Jesus pointed down the ladder and said, "*If you think I'm great, be a reflection of me. I came to serve, so go and serve likewise. That's greatness.*" Jesus said that the secret to living a "successful" life (if He'd even use that word) is to serve others.

He emphasized that we don't shine through getting approval or promotions, but through giving (life, love, hope) away. The most effective way to shine in God's kingdom is not to strive harder and climb higher, but to bend low and humbly to meet the needs of others.

## THE SERVANT COMPETITION LIE

Since serving is at the crux of how God designed us to shine, the Enemy would like nothing more than to twist our desire to serve God into another way to measure our worth. So he tries to sneak yet another lie into our hearts that we have to out-serve someone else to be sure we matter to God.

Lately, as God's been planting new dreams in my heart to serve others, I'm hyper-aware of all the amazing kingdom servants around me. There are people almost half my age who seem to have completely surpassed me in servant-worth. They've started organizations on behalf of the poor and suffering. They've turned their massive twitter platform into an opportunity to raise money for charities and hope. They speak at a national level and they never seem to have a bad hair day. They are so servant-shiny that there's no way I can keep up.

But Jesus doesn't have a bar graph showing which areas of serving matter more to the kingdom. He simply says, "*Serve. Take in a stranger. Give someone a cup of water in my name. If someone is hungry, feed him. If someone curses you, bless them. Love.*"

We don't have to compare our cup of water to someone else's- we just give it away. The more confident we are in God's love for us, the more serving becomes a natural reflection of who He is instead of yet another list of things we need to do to matter or make God happy.

We should ask God to show us where we might be making excuses for ourselves to avoid getting our hands dirty in serving. Serving isn't always glamorous and will require sacrifice by nature.

When we feel like our serving is a gauge of our worth, we're likely to focus on "official serving" at a major charity event, church ministry, or missions trip. But serving happens primarily in the everyday, without necessarily being commissioned or even noticed by anyone but God.

Serving is my friend washing my dishes while I put my kids to bed because she knows it will give me joy. Serving is my sister being a daily person of hope through relationships with local teens as she teaches art and theater. Serving is my husband spending an afternoon teaching my kids to play that video game he picked out for them. Serving is addressing poverty one person at a time by offering to pay for music lessons for the kid who can't afford them.

When we view certain serving opportunities as shinier or more important than others, we're actually missing the heart of God's desire for us to serve in every circumstance. Serving isn't something you sign up for; it's a way of life.

This is a key distinction, because we're all in different life seasons with different backgrounds and talents. We're all in process to being made more like God, and there's nothing that kills serving more than comparing your servant level or position to someone else.

God is more concerned with our hearts to serve everyone we encounter in love than in whether our serving has measurable results in this world. God's kingdom simply can't be quantified through all the statistics, data, and numbers we'd like to process our efforts through.

Just go. Serve the people in your path today. And don't worry if it doesn't feel like much. Be sensitive to God and as you step out and serve in small areas, He'll lead you to more. If He wants you to do more, trust that He'll convict you.

Once we confront the lies in our own worlds, we need to counter those lies with the lens of serving out of love. It may sound too easy, but if you begin to filter all of your stress about how to matter through the filter of a loving servant, you'll find so much freedom and clarity. As a loved and valued child of God, you're free to shine through giving back what you've been freely given, without worrying that your worth will ever run out in giving yourself away.

As a mom, every action, whether cooking a meal, arbitrating the hundredth argument of the day or making time to be silly with my kids, is an act of serving. There's so much more joy in even the mundane tasks in my life (read: washing dishes) when I view them as gifts of service rather than measures of my worth.

As a writer I don't shine more by racking up more followers and book sales, but by asking how I can serve my readers and listeners. *"God, how can I serve people?"* is a far more liberating and purposeful question than *"Does someone like me?"* or *"Do I matter to this person?"* Shining to serve in love eliminates the need to collect other people's opinions of us. I simply need to ask how I can meet a need. Who is right next to me today that I can lift up?

Go low to glow: to reflect Jesus as a moon means to humbly follow His servant heart.

## THOSE LIVING IN DARKNESS

My kids love flashlights. I'm not sure if they're more excited about the ability to control a light or the opportunity to blind people's eyes. They use a flashlight to create a spotlight in their made up theatrical performances, and they bring my phone flashlight deep inside their blanket forts to read or write. But the irony is, they don't ever want to be in a situation where they legitimately need a flashlight.

Flashlights are great as accessories when there's plenty of other lights already shining, but the minute the power in our house goes out at night, my kids are completely panicked. They forget that those same flashlights they love to play with were actually designed for just such a storm-induced darkness. But once we get the flashlight on, they experience the fullness of its purpose as it pushes against the enveloping ebony around them.

In the same way, God tells us that we're meant to shine like a city on a hill. And while we're told to love and care for our brothers and sisters in Christ, we're especially called to be the light of the world as Jesus is. (Matthew 5:14)

We aren't just called to be a light where light is already prevalent; we're meant to seek out those living in darkness as we once were. God's incredible glory on display isn't meant to keep to ourselves or to boost our value, but to illuminate and restore a broken world. We can only light up the world by being brave enough to walk in its midst.

Love146 (www.love146.org) is an organization that knows a thing or two about walking in darkness. Co-founder Rob Morris shares the gut wrenching story of a trip to Southeast Asia to assess how he could be part of ending child trafficking in that area and beyond. They couldn't bring light until they'd immersed themselves into the needs of a dark reality.

Morris describes one investigative trip to a brothel to help free girls: "We found ourselves standing shoulder to shoulder with predators in a small room, looking at young girls through a pane of glass. All of the girls wore red dresses with a number pinned to their dress for identification.[1]"

He describes how each girl had a visible numbness to her countenance from the despair and trauma of being used night after night by different men. Yet one girl, who wore the number "146" still had fight in her eyes, as darkness but not being able to rescue this small girl yet.

"All of these emotions begin to wreck you. Break you. It is agony. It is aching. It is grief. It is sorrow. The reaction is intuitive, instinctive. It is visceral. It releases a wailing cry inside of you. It elicits gut-level indignation. It is unbearable. I remember wanting to break through the glass. To take her away from that place. To scoop up as many of them as I could into my arms. To take all of them away. I wanted to break through the glass to tell her to keep fighting. To not give up. To tell her that we were coming for her.[2]"

Though many from that brothel were ultimately freed, the precious girl with the number "146" was no longer there at the time of the rescue. Words can't describe the heartbreak when darkness seems to win. But Morris and others believed strongly that the only way the dark could truly win, would be if the light turned its back on the night. And they refused. Instead, out of that incredible darkness, they birthed light.

The story of one girl trapped in darkness became the catalyst for a movement of love. When naming their organization, they found a way to transform the very symbol of darkness into a beacon of hope. I can't put it any better than Love146 does: "Her name became a number. Her number became our name.[3]"

Today Love146 has two survivor care facilities for trafficking victims in the Philippines, and programs for survivors in the US and UK as well. They've even begun a prevention program in Africa. In addition, they provide extensive trafficking prevention education in schools, raise awareness of what trafficking is and how to respond, and create communities of dedicated anti-trafficking volunteers.

Morris and the staff at Love146 today realize that as painful as it is to experience the hurt and ache of the darkness, that's precisely where the light is meant to shine.

Sometimes the darkness looks like the evil of trafficking children for sex. Other times it looks like generational poverty, the heartbreak of the foster care system, addictions, bullying, systemic racism and inequality. We can't combat all of these things personally, but we are called to care about all of them because God cares about all injustice.

We're meant to take up our piece of the darkness, the places where God allows our hearts to be broken as His is, and run towards change. Pursue justice. In Isaiah 58:6-8, God promises us that as we pursue His heart for injustice, our light will break forth:

"Is not this the kind of fasting I have chosen:
  to loose the chains of injustice
    and untie the cords of the yoke,
  to set the oppressed free
    and break every yoke?
 Is it not to share your food with the hungry
    and to provide the poor wanderer with shelter—
 when you see the naked, to clothe them,
    and not to turn away from your own flesh and blood?
 Then *your light will break forth like the dawn,*
    and your healing will quickly appear;
 then your righteousness will go before you,
    and *the glory of the Lord will be your rear guard.*" [italics mine]

Our light appears when we pursue freedom for others- which goes back to our idea of serving. While the passage specifically talks about helping the hungry and homeless and our families, I love that verse six tells us that we're meant to "break every yoke."

The closest I've gotten to living off the land is struggling to grow supposedly easy veggies like tomatoes and squash in my garden plot. Most of my plants don't make it very far, so I don't claim to be an expert in farming.

But I did read *Little House on the Prairie*, so I know that a yoke is what you put around the oxen's neck to control them and harness them to a plow. I don't even like to wear turtlenecks, so a yoke sounds pretty uncomfortable. But more than that, the yoke is symbolic of the heavy work the oxen must accomplish. An ox that is yoked is at the whim of his master- he isn't free.

So when we're told to "break every yoke" it's this powerful image to find anything that is keeping someone from freedom, and work with God to break that yoke or chain off of them. Going into the darkness to pursue justice isn't just about temporarily lifting someone up, it's about breaking off the systems and circumstances that are keeping them bound in the dark. That's justice. And that's when our light shines, because that's when we're reflecting God's heart for justice as moons were made to do.

Sometimes meeting the darkness and breaking yokes requires us to do as Rob Morris did and create an organization to combat the evil. In this way we come alongside others and build a powerful community of change. Organizations create momentum and strategy for lifting many people out of their oppression. But we should never forget that walking into the darkness isn't about helping a faceless mass of people, but about real individuals with unique stories.

We are just as needed and significant if we are serving one person or a million. Our journey into the darkness requires us to start paying attention not just to the large scale problems of oppression, but the individual stories of oppression that we only learn through one-on-one interactions. Sometimes facing the dark is walking down the street to talk to a neighbor. Sometimes it's looking into the face of one homeless person and letting them tell you their story.

A good friend of mine found herself deeply broken by the refugee crisis. She could have simply donated to a refugee agency or retweeted statistics on the welfare of refugee families. But instead, she looked for a way to connect with an actual refugee family in her town. While she has given so much to this family, she says she's received so much as well. Because she chose to be with someone and listen to them, she physically brought hope and light instead of just talking about it. We need those individual encounters as well as the large scale movements to collectively break chains off of people.

And as we do, God promises not only that our light will break forth, but that his glory will "be our rear guard." (vs. 8) This is an astounding image for us as moons. It's as though God wraps us up in His light. He will shine where we are incapable of glowing because His light is beyond anything we could manipulate or comprehend.

It really is all about Him. As we address the lies we believe about how we are meant to shine, and step out to serve and free others from the darkness, we become agents of God's hope in the dark.

## MOON UNIVERSITY
### Lesson Five

**Star Lie #5**: Go up to shine. Out-serve to matter. Be followed to shine.

**Moon Truth #5**: Go low to shine. You shine brightest in the dark. Be a servant to shine.

Question 1: What are the "star lies" you're tempted to believe in your own life? What makes you feel like you matter in your current roles?

Question 2: Are there certain people you find yourself constantly trying to get validation from?

Question 3: Think of all the ways Jesus lived opposite to the world's version of success. Does this challenge the way you've been living?

Question 4: Be intentional about serving in small ways this week. Who has God put in your path that you can serve with no strings attached?

Question 5: What did you think of the story of Rob Morris and Love146? Can you think of other examples of people who walked in the darkness in order to bring powerful light to others?

Question 6: What are some "chains" or "yokes" of oppression that you see around you in the world? How might God want to use you to break those chains? Take a baby step (ex. start a conversation, look up a website, familiarize yourself with a problem) to see the needs of the dark this week.

# 6
# AVOIDING AN ECLIPSE

"Love must be sincere. Hate what is evil; cling to what is good. Be devoted to one another in love. Honor one another above yourselves."
**-Romans 12:9-10**

"'Be still, and know that I am God;
   I will be exalted among the nations,
   I will be exalted in the earth.'"
   **-Psalm 46:10**

## LUNAR ECLIPSE

I've always been the girl who wanted to rise above the clichés of my gender and prove to all you guys out there that I could keep up. I remember trying to chow down two burgers as a kid simply because my dad could. As a young teenager, I challenged one of my guy friends to an arm wrestling match and beat him with my secret weapon: left-handedness. (I actually kind of liked that guy; but apparently the way to a guy's heart isn't through beating him in a strength contest.)

Though I'm still a champion of women's strength today, I do have a rather lady-like confession: I'm all about chick flicks. One of my favorites is *How to Lose a Guy in 10 Days*, where Kate Hudson plays a woman trying to work her way up as a writer in the magazine world. In an endeavor to help her dating-challenged friend while simultaneously impressing her boss, she decides to write an article about all the ways women drive men away.

To complete her how not-to-date segment, she must choose a guy to date then get him to dump her using only the typical pitfalls women make. Comedy ensues as she attempts everything from making a fake photobook of their future child together, to intentionally interrupting his guys-only poker night. Matthew McConaughey plays her experimental date whose patience is stretched thinner with each new intentional faux pas.

Though not the most thought-provoking film ever, the movie does illustrate an important point as we continue in learning how to be a moon: part of shining is learning how not to shine. Now that we know what it means to shine God's way, we'd be wise to ask ourselves if there's anything that can actually keep us from reflecting God fully.

In the natural world, historically there's just one event that has kept the moon from shining. We refer to this phenomenon as a lunar eclipse, when the moon passes directly into the shadow of the Earth. The only thing that can keep our beautiful satellite from shining is if the Earth comes between the moon and its light source.

As moons reflecting God, the same is true of us; when we start fixating on the world instead of our Sun, we're in trouble. Just as the Earth can create a shadow over the moon, so the world and its values can eclipse our view of God if we let it.

Let me be clear: God will never forsake or abandon us. There have been times when I've let the world dim God's light in my life, and unfortunately it will happen again. This is why God asks us to take up our cross daily, because the decision to follow God isn't a one time thing, but an ongoing choice to submit.

Yet the beauty of God's unchanging, unfailing love is that even when we aren't fully turned towards Him, He is always fully turned towards us. Our distraction and even disobedience don't change our identity as God's, but they absolutely hurt us.

The world's light is loss because it promises satisfaction but doesn't follow through. My friend says processed food is that way. These foods are engineered to create a tantalizing experience which leaves a person always wanting more but never fully satisfied. Food companies sell more food if you never quite feel like you've had enough. In the same way, the world dangles a carrot of validation, joy, and pleasure in front of us, but always just out of reach.

More than that, whatever light we pursue apart from Christ is actually darkness. Isaiah 50:10-11 says,

"Let the one who walks in the dark, who has no light, trust in the name of the Lord and rely on their God. But now, all you who light fires and provide yourselves with flaming torches, go, walk in the light of your fires and of the torches you have set ablaze. This is what you shall receive from my hand: You will lie down in torment."

"Torment" kind of screams at me there. It's a bit harsh, God, don't you think? I'd like to smooth down its harsh edges and say that God must have meant a tamer word like "discomfort" or perhaps "disappointment." But then again, if we're trusting in anything other than God, aren't we walking towards the opposite of what He alone can give?

If He gives peace, pure and unadulterated, then torment is the logical opposite. The light we try to scrounge up for ourselves, our futile attempts to walk in the world's light, can only lead to misery, striving, and dissatisfaction.

Contrast this feeling to the sentiment of the Psalmist in Psalm 17:15: "As for me, I will be vindicated and will see your face; when I awake, I will be satisfied with seeing your likeness." Satisfaction comes from staring in the face of Jesus, knowing Him and His light. When we focus on the world, we forfeit the path of peace He offers.

But the final reason it's so dangerous to let the world's lies keep us from seeking God's face, is that it keeps us from lighting up the very world by which we're mesmerized. That's exactly what the current prince of this world, our Enemy, is banking on.

The Enemy, that father of lies who prowls to devour us like a lion, started off as another beautiful creation of God. But then he bought all-in to the one simple lie that he could actually be brighter without God. Outside of Him. In his own merit. Maybe he could be more than the Creator's best. If we think that the world's lies are no big deal, we should know that every one of them originated with the one whose goal is to steal from, kill, and destroy us.

He works best in darkness, so he'd like to keep the world in the dark. The evil and brokenness that are so prevalent are his brainchild. Yet he can't compete with the inexhaustible light of Christ! That light is always more powerful than the dark, able to renew and restore, able to offer hope and a future where only death seemed possible.

If Christ could rewrite His own death into redemption for humanity, then there simply are no longer limits for what His light can do. The Enemy hates the thought of God's people magnifying and scattering light throughout the world he's trying to black out.

Our Enemy knows he can't shut down our Light Source, so he's out to find any way of getting between us and Christ. He's used different tactics and angles through the years, but I believe one of the most lethal lies has been saved for this generation.

The Enemy knows how deeply we want to change the world for good by shining like stars in our generation. But he's infiltrated our desire to shine for God and filled it with his own poison so we pursue bright in all the wrong ways. If our antagonist can just keep us running after significance, trying to grow our followings, wondering whether we're bright enough yet for God, then we'll lose sight of God Himself.

## THREE SIGNS OF STAR LIES

There are three key characteristics that plague us when we buy into the Enemy's star lies: pride, envy, and selfish ambition. Sure, you could make an exhaustive list of slimy, evil characteristics of Satan and his lies (not a great date night activity) but I believe most of his deceit falls into these three characteristics.

First John 2:15-16 says, "Do not love the world or anything in the world. If anyone loves the world, love for the Father is not in them. For everything in the world—the lust of the flesh, the lust of the eyes, and the pride of life—comes not from the Father but from the world."

Pride is a function of loving the world, of focusing on the world's beliefs. Pride can cause us to believe that we simply don't need God, that we can accumulate more worth without Him. The minute we believe that, we stop seeking God's light and try to create our own like stars.

What does pride look like in your life? For me, pride is believing that an idea is really mine (not God's) and trying to keep others from using my idea without giving me credit. Pride looks like finding everyone else's problems, but conveniently ignoring my own sinful heart. Pride is my belief that other people owe me, that I deserve more (accolades, opportunities, stickers on my reward chart) because of who I am and what I've done. Pride is when I become more interested in how the world sees ME than whether the world sees my awesome God.

Pride is directly related to envy and selfish ambition as well. James 3:14-16 says, "But if you harbor bitter envy and selfish ambition in your hearts, do not boast about it or deny the truth. Such 'wisdom' does not come down from heaven but is earthly, unspiritual, demonic. For where you have envy and selfish ambition, there you find disorder and every evil practice."

We might look at the end of that verse and think that James got just a wee bit over-dramatic there for a minute. I mean, I've been known to make a dramatic statement or 2,000 in my lifetime, so I should know. Are envy and selfish ambition really demonic attributes at the heart of every evil practice?

But if you stop to boil down the evils of the world, it actually makes sense. We want something and can't have it so we justify more and more until we get what we want.

Even in the Biblical story where Cain kills Abel, the murder grows out of simple selfish ambition. Abel has approval that Cain doesn't have and he uses that desire to fuel and justify murder. Selfish ambition can be at the heart of everything from theft and lies to rape and genocide. That sounds like darkness to me. When pride causes us to elevate our ambition over God's, we can justify just about anything in pursuit of ourselves.

I have to daily check the pulse of my motives, because even good things can become self-focused if our hearts are left unattended. Even while writing this book and seeking more speaking engagements, I've had to ask myself if I'm ultimately seeking my glory or God's. Because if speaking or writing is my end goal, then it's about me. If my end goal is to know and be with Jesus, then it doesn't actually matter what accomplishments wait at the finish line.

Moses teaches us what it means to pursue God to the exclusion of any other task or ambition. When God told Moses to lead His people into he Promised Land, Moses didn't start making a strategic plan of conquer. He didn't allow his significant role to become His god. Instead, he replied honestly that he simply wouldn't move forward if God's presence wasn't going with them. (Exodus 33:15) Moses knew that there's no destination, no ambition, no promise, that outweighs God Himself.

As we seek God's presence, He reminds us of his counter-worldly truth. God says not to look out to our own interests alone, but also to the needs of others. God says to consider others as better than ourselves. (Philippians 2:3-4) He says love our neighbor as ourselves. (Matthew 22:39) Following these precepts keeps our hearts rooted in God's kingdom, staving off the lies of the Enemy.

Finally, we must guard our hearts against envy, which is a symptom of believing that God didn't make us equal or doesn't love us equally. It's at the heart of the lie that we have to do more, be more, try harder to be enough. Envy keeps us ineffective and fractured as believers. We can't possibly be working together as one in love if we're too busy competing for sufficiency that was ours all along.

Jesus said, "If a house is divided against itself, that house cannot stand." (Mark 3:25) Envy is one powerful way the enemy causes foundation-shaking division in our homes, churches, workplaces, and communities. Envy clouds our united vision, draws lines between us and those we should be working alongside, and silences love in the name of competition.

Envy was a core problem in my opening story about wanting to be more important on the worship team. Though I was friends with each of the other singers, jealousy had poisoned my thinking in ways I didn't realize till later. In one season, when I was rarely scheduled to sing at church, I found myself wrestling each week, envious of the other girls. Sometimes they'd sing an ideal low song, and I'd think to myself that I could have sung it just as well, or better. I could totally be worshipping like a boss.

But nobody was keeping me from worshipping...except me and my envy. I'd allowed envy to move in between me and my ability to be led by my sisters in Christ to worship the One who gave each of us our voices for Himself.

God was faithful to show me the cesspool in my soul and the way it was poisoning me. Slowly I surrendered, and at some point the envy began to lift. After a while, I discovered that I was able to simply enjoy the beautiful worship of another creation doing what she was designed to do. I allowed myself to believe that active envy might eventually produce some results for me. The only thing it excelled at was stealing my joy.

I still struggle at times, wishing I had her platform or his role. But I've discovered the freedom of calling envy out and allowing God to produce an ability to enjoy others instead.

Where have envy and selfish ambition thrown themselves at you? Do you feel the need to wear the latest fashion or slim down just a little more to be loved? Do you find you're willing to let someone else take the fall for a mistake you made so you can inch ahead? Do you struggle to be happy for others when they do well? If you're honest, are you more driven by the desire to be noticed or applauded than by your desire to serve others?

I've been there so many times, and the truth is these lies aren't just going to disappear one day like a dozen freshly baked cookies. As long as we live in this world we will have trouble- but Jesus also promises He's overcome the world. So how can we stand in God's truth and power and overcome the lies of the world? I think this calls for a story about coffee.

## WHY STRIVING IS KILLING OUR JOY

Getting my children out the door requires the discipline of an Olympic endurance sport athlete. My three year old spills mischievous laughter all over the floor along with whatever toys he can throw. I bark upstairs to my seven year old, asking if he's dressed, and he emerges with last night's Ironman pajamas and his favorite excuse: "I got distracted."

I glance at my eight year old, slumped on the couch, devouring another chapter book. "Are you ready to go, Sweetie?" I query. She answers "yes" without looking up from her reading, and I stare at her suspiciously shoeless feet. "You don't have anything else to put on?"

This particular morning of trying to pack kids in the car was no different than usual and, fun fact, I do not have the discipline of an Olympic endurance athlete. In fact, I had to google "endurance athlete" just to make sure it was a real thing. So in the midst of the chaos of partially dressed children waiting to be corralled, I did what any dedicated mother would do: I swiped my phone to check for emails or messages or really any contact with the outside world. And the phone cosmos rewarded me with a text from a friend:

*"Can you meet for coffee today at 10:00 am?"*

I'd been excited about this tentative coffee plan for a while. As a mom, I savor any chance to have deep discussions with real live adults. The text

64

was an invitation to meet up with good friends of mine to brainstorm for our church's Christmas service. Nothing gets you in the Christmas frame of mind like a Starbucks coffee outing in the middle of July.

I agreed to meet because, frankly, I'd be willing to discuss migratory patterns of insects if free coffee is involved. Plus creative planning is right up my alley, and somehow the invitation to join these kinds of projects always makes me feel validated and valuable. (Hello, Pride!)

But getting coffee today at 10:00? Well that simply wouldn't work since- reality check!- I was in the middle of yelling my kids into the van to get my son to a 9:30 doctor's appointment. But when I'm banking on a Christmas-coffee-planning meeting to feel validated and valuable, my brain launches into irrational self-preservation mode.

So I counter-texted that I could meet at 10:30 if we could move the location to the coffee shop near my pediatrician. Nice, Carrye, quick thinking. Never mind that I would have all my kids with me and wouldn't be able to focus. Details.

Then I got the deal-breaker: the two of them had some additional things to go over, so they'd meet at ten today at the coffee shop in the opposite direction, and perhaps I could meet another time. Maybe next week. But if you haven't heard, next week isn't for people who are needed today! Today my friend was clearly destined to play a more important role than me. (And there's envy, right on schedule.)

While still processing my apparent defeat, my friend texted to ask if her husband could watch my kids so I could still join. My mind, ever tripping on its need for control, warped this offer of childcare into an irrational renewed glimmer of hope. Within a moment I hatched the ridiculous plan that went something like this: I would march my son to his appointment, probably late, and hope the doctor finished by 10:00. I could then coax my children back into the car with some form of confectionary bribery, and drive the twenty minutes back towards home.

Then I'd simply drop my sugar-hyped offspring at my friend's house, hop back in the van and drive another twenty minutes to the coffee meeting. Of course I'd be an hour late and would also have to give up the grocery trip I'd planned. But how much do my kids really need milk and bread and meat and vegetables? That's why we have multi-vitamins.

I started to text my friends back with my brilliant new solution, but then I stopped because my brain was hyperventilating at the precariously stacked crazy I'd devised. I realized that the fear of missing out and possibly losing my value footing was actually making me strive the fun right out of my day. (Because that's what pride and envy do.) It was poisoning my joy. So I pried my fingers off the remote control, agreeing to meet whenever "next time" might be, even if I wasn't quite so critical a piece in the planning.

As I drove my kids to my son's appointment, I prayed, "*God, what lie am*

*I believing that makes me feel the need to strive and clutch at even small places of significance?"*

And the answer could be one of so many lies at the root of our journey. Do I not trust that my worth is secure no matter what? Do I not believe that God has a plan to create with me today wherever I go? Do I trust more in the importance people assign me than the importance God bestows?

Right around three miles from my house, my whole being started re-absorbing His truth about who I am and what I'm worth. The fresh breeze swirled through the open van windows, and my heart briefly felt it could float with that wind. From that place of freedom, I recognized my desire to strive for the sinister trap it was: an insatiable self-imposed quest that bound me with weariness, stress, and false worth. But when I confronted my lies and surrendered them to God, He was able to plant joy and rest where striving had been.

## CONFORMED VS TRANSFORMED

Our orbit around the Earth's lies is so daily. We want to be powerfully used by God to meet needs in the darkness, yet the very place we're meant to shine great hope becomes our greatest temptation. Over and over again we're pulled towards the Earth like the very gravity that holds the moon in place.

Occasionally we reach a plateau where we feel that we've finally moved beyond the world's pull. At times I really believed I'd overcome my jealousy of people who were doing the things I wished I could be doing. There were moments I really felt content to just be in the presence of God forever, come what may.

But inevitably, we loop back through those feelings of inadequacy, jealousy, pride and ambition. Each of us has unique triggers that arouse negative feelings in us, often taking us by surprise.

Maybe someone goes off on a praise-rave about another singer or artist right in front of your nose. Comparison. Maybe the new person in your group is wildly successful at everything he tries while you feel like you're failing. Jealousy. Maybe you suddenly get a spike in blog readers or Instagram followers and your heart starts desiring more recognition. Selfish-ambition. Perhaps you were seeking to honor God with your ability or career but when the accolades came pouring in, you started subtly believing you were responsible for your success. Pride.

Where are you prone to look to the world for validation? What lies of shining are likely to block you from fixing your eyes on Jesus?

You may not want to hear this, but if you're someone who seems to struggle over and over to fight against the world's lies, you are just so...normal.

Paul talks about our ongoing wrestling with the desires of our flesh in a passage you've probably heard many times: "So I find this law at work: Although I want to do good, evil is right there with me. For in my inner being I delight in God's law; but I see another law at work in me, waging war against the law of my mind and making me a prisoner of the law of sin at work within me." (Romans 7:21-23)

There's a tug-of-war going on constantly between the desires of the world and of God. We really do want God and His ways, but we get discouraged because we can't seem to shake this broken flesh. But rather than looking at our daily wrestle with the world as a disqualification from serving God, I'd like to suggest we can use it as a tool to help us.

God says "Do not conform to the pattern of this world, but be transformed by the renewing of your mind." (Romans 12:2) With each temptation that arises, we can be conformed, or transformed: conformed to the world's lies, or transformed by God's truth.

When you feel a strong temptation towards striving, pride, envy, or selfish ambition, try to view them as spiritual barometers letting you know where your heart needs work. Don't walk in guilt because these struggles crop up; instead, realize that they're just symptoms of the deeper lies that the enemy wants to ingrain in us.

Remember, you have a choice about how you respond to those lies. When we act on the world's lies we allow ourselves to be conformed by them and shape our behavior. That leads us towards all kinds of heartache. But instead of acting on those lies, we can give them to God and allow Him to transform our thinking to align with His heart and truth. Can you imagine how much stress, striving, false-worth, and fear we'd drop if we let Him transform us more often?

And though my coffee story may seem trivial, sometimes the trivial places are the best times to practice this experiment of letting God renew our minds. Then when something bigger comes, like being let go from a job, being abandoned by a spouse or friends, or getting a rejection letter from a school or publisher- your mind will be better trained to rest in who God has made you to be in spite of the hurt.

I'm not a formula person because I believe God works uniquely in each of us. But there's power in looking at the temptations in our lives through a "conformed" vs. "transformed" mindset. For those who enjoy a little practical application, here are some basic steps for allowing God to speak through your daily temptations. To help you remember, I'll borrow the public service announcement acronym **P.S.A.**: **P**ay Attention, **S**urrender, and **A**sk.

1.  **P**ay attention to your strong or irrational emotions.

It could be those times when your reaction to an event or circumstance feels out of proportion with the circumstance itself. For instance, my frantic reaction to the minor problem of being unable to attend my friends' coffee meeting. Ahem.

Identify whether you feel anger, pride, fear, insecurity, etc. Pinpointing what you're feeling helps you overcome its grip. You may find that these feelings occur most frequently in specific situations or around specific people.

It can be helpful to make a note of those things so that you're more aware of your future weak spots. Second Peter 2:19 says, "people are slaves to whatever has mastered them." So the question is, will you let these emotions/reactions master you, or will you move on to the next step and surrender them?

2.  **S**urrender your heart and emotions to God, ugly and all.

Don't hold back because He already knows your heart and loves you anyway. Ask Him to show you what lies are fueling your strong feeling. What lies are your temptations symptoms of?

For example: God, I'm feeling very irritable and stressed about finishing this project. Please show me if I'm believing or acting on lies that are stealing my joy.

OR: God I felt really offended when I wasn't asked to help plan the event because I've always done that well in the past. It really hurts. Please show me if I'm listening to a lie that's keeping my heart from your peace.

Paul says in 1 Corinthians 10:13 that "No temptation has overtaken you except what is common to mankind. And God is faithful; he will not let you be tempted beyond what you can bear. But when you are tempted, he will also provide a way out so that you can endure it."

Our temptations are common, which means we're not alone in our struggles. And yet God's faithful nature never wavers, and He's ready to provide and equip us with renewal of our minds if we ask Him.

3.  **A**sk God to remind you of His truth about you and your situation.

Ask God to give you verses, or print out a list of verses ahead of time that scream the truth. This is how God transforms your worldly thinking into His kingdom mentality. God whispers over you that you are His child, that He had kingdom plans for you before you were born. God reminds you that it was never up to you to accomplish success or glory for yourself, because He has accomplished it all for you with His hand and His power.

It's not easy and God's truth isn't a magic wand to remove all pain or struggle from your circumstances. We're going to keep wrestling. But God makes us a powerful promise in 2 Corinthians 3:16-18:

> "But whenever anyone turns to the Lord, the veil is taken away. Now the Lord is the Spirit, and where the Spirit of the Lord is, there is freedom. And we all, who with unveiled faces contemplate the Lord's glory, are being transformed into his image with ever-increasing glory, which comes from the Lord, who is the Spirit."

Did you notice the continued moon-reflection metaphor here? I love it. This verse is reminding us that as we simply turn towards God, His Spirit begins to open us to God's truth. And as we enter the freedom of His presence and contemplate HIS glory, we are transformed into His image.

Know this: the fruit of our transformed souls has eternal consequences that will far outweigh any success or accolade here on earth. Every step away from pride, envy, and selfish ambition is a step towards reflecting God more powerfully. One of the first fruits we'll find in ditching pride, envy and selfish ambition is an increased joy in shining in community.

# MOON UNIVERSITY
## Lesson Six

**Star Lie #6**: The fame, success, and pleasure of this world will satisfy you completely.

**Moon Truth #6**: Chasing the world always ends in emptiness and keeps you from fully reflecting God's heart.

Question 1: Where do you see pride, envy, or selfish ambition at work in your life? How are they robbing you of true joy and freedom?

Question 2: After reading my story about missing coffee with friends, can you think of a time in your life when you felt desperate to be included or needed? What did you do?

Question 3: Discuss the idea of "conformed" vs. "transformed". How might the P.S.A. steps help you in a specific situation in your life? If that exercise didn't connect with you, can you think of another way to help you recognize lies of significance and act on truth?

# 7
# GLORY IN COMMUNITY

"Do not think of yourself more highly than you ought, but rather think of yourself with sober judgment, in accordance with the faith God has distributed to each of you. For just as each of us has one body with many members, and these members do not all have the same function,  so in Christ we, though many, form one body, and each member belongs to all the others."
**-Romans 12:3-5**

## LEARNING TO SHARE GLORY

Sharing comes naturally to some people, but I'm not "some people." I'm irrationally possessive of my personal-sized fuzzy blanket, I make lame excuses when my daughter asks to wear my favorite jewelry, and I avoid sharing driving time on fourteen hour trips to visit my parents. (That steering wheel is mine!)

Of all the things I hate to share, food is at the top of my list.  Two of my best friends are constantly co-ordering food, giddy in their excitement to divide and swap bites of risotto and fish or flourless chocolate cake.  I order my carb-friendly food for me, myself and I, thank you very much. I'm like Joey from the TV show *Friends*, who gets mad at his date for ordering her own food then trying to nibble some of his.  I could easily steal his line for myself: "Carrye doesn't share food!"

Food-hoarding might be a superficial selfishness, but if I'm honest my struggle to share is often far more malignant.  As a fellow moon-in-training, one of my biggest obstacles is learning to share glory.  I know that all I have is grace, but I wrestle in glory-tension.  When God gives me any kind of platform to reflect Him I'm excited to serve those around me, but I also desire to hold onto that shine for myself to feel important.

Your platform may be anything but a stage. Maybe as a leader you're nervous to mentor someone younger who might excel in his gifts and leave you feeling somewhat obsolete. Maybe you're one step ahead of a co-worker and you fear that if you give them encouragement or advice, they'll take it with a smile and edge ahead of you for that promotion. Maybe you're overwhelmed by always cooking the Thanksgiving feast but you're afraid of sharing that role with your sister because she's good at everything and cooking made you stand out.

I get it. Stars have been known to catch their death from glory-sharing. So instead, we glory-hog. Like basketball players protecting the ball, we own our place on the court and thrust our elbows out to claim our territory. We need to be needed. We think we can control our value by serving through our own gifts, but not necessarily going out of our way to invest in other people's gifts or share glory-space.

The problem for moons is that holding onto glory is counterproductive. God's glory is designed to be interactive, growing in power as it is given away. God magnifies and multiplies His glory through relationships.

If we want to see reciprocal glory at its best, we need look no further than how God interacts within Himself. On the eve of his death, we find Jesus praying in the crushing loneliness of the Garden of Gethsemane. Just as people lean in close to breathe in every syllable of a dying friend or relative, we can draw close to Jesus and learn powerful truth from some of His final words on earth with God.

> "'Father, the hour has come. Glorify your Son, that your Son may glorify you. For you granted him authority over all people that he might give eternal life to all those you have given him. Now this is eternal life: that they know you, the only true God, and Jesus Christ, whom you have sent. I have brought you glory on earth by finishing the work you gave me to do. And now, Father, glorify me in your presence with the glory I had with you before the world began." (John 17:1-5)

God, in the mystery of three persons, shared glory in relationship before the beginning of time. When Jesus came to earth, He intentionally gave up some of His God-glory in choosing to become human. Yet even in weak human body, He brought glory to God through His obedience. And He knew that even as He carried shameful death on the cross, God would yet glorify Him even more powerfully through resurrection and honor in His kingdom. God is all-glorious, and yet His own glory was magnified through give and take within Himself.

Pause a minute to take that in.

If Jesus Himself was glory-sharing with the Father, how much more are we meant to go and do likewise as His children?

Obviously there are some differences between us and Jesus. (I'm pretty sure I just heard someone say "Amen!") We don't manufacture or claim any right to the glory that God gives us. Yet we do give shared glory back to God in relationship, dancing with our Maker, as we live out what He's called us to do here on earth.

This pattern of glory-sharing within the Trinity is also a call for how we're meant to share and magnify glory in relationship with other humans. Stars are afraid to share glory because their worth is threatened by other bright lights. But moons understand there is no shining unless someone else is willing to share their glory with you. As a result, when we lead others to know and reflect Jesus, they become part of our glory too. We don't have to be afraid of investing in others, because our glory is relationally collective.

Paul explains this well in an affectionate letter to the church at Thessalonica. He writes "as a father deals with his own children, encouraging, comforting and urging you to live lives worthy of God, who calls you into his kingdom and glory." (1 Thessalonians 2:11-12)

In all the witnessing, exhortation, and affection, Paul feels that, like spiritual children, the Thessalonians are a reflection of His own love and hard work. Therefore, he says confidently, "For what is our hope, our joy, or the crown in which we will glory in the presence of our Lord Jesus when he comes? Is it not you? Indeed, you are our glory and joy." (vs. 19-20)

Paul doesn't say that he feels brighter and more significant around the Thessalonians because they're a reflection of him. He says they themselves are his glory. When he stands before Jesus in the end, his heart won't swell with pride from a list of accomplishments or the number of times he put his life on the line for God (and for Paul that number is pretty high).

His reflected glory was beautifully wrapped up in those he served, and likewise their reflected glory was magnified as they loved beyond themselves. Our glory isn't possessive, but relational. We're all in a giant glory triangle (or whatever shape millions of us create) with God.

## MIRRORING GOD'S CREATIVE WORD

All this talk of relational glory is giving me a vague warm fuzzy feeling, like I'm singing and laughing around a campfire with friends on a crisp October evening with a toasty beverage. Somebody is wearing button-up plaid flannel and a hat with Sherpa lined ear flaps; another person's face is barely visible from inside their fleece-blanket cocoon, and there's one stubborn hold-out wearing a holey sweatshirt with shorts and flip flops. But he's got a guitar to keep him warm.

While I love this image, sharing our shine with one another goes far beyond mutual affection and cozy togetherness. It's not all breezy joy; it's a sacrifice and it just might sting. Yet living out relational glory is a sobering task we've been entrusted with that we must intentionally pursue. That requires us to look yet again to our Maker to see how He shares glory through investing in us.

Since God's glory investment in us began at creation, we can go back to the beginning to get an idea of how we're meant to invest in others. As an author, I love that John refers to Jesus as "the Word":

"In the beginning was the Word, and the Word was with God, and the Word was God. He was with God in the beginning. Through him all things were made; without him nothing was made that has been made. In him was life, and that life was the light of all mankind. The light shines in the darkness, and the darkness has not overcome it."
(John 1:1-6)

This passage not only continues our theme of Jesus as Light in the darkness, but also brings up a metaphor for Jesus that will help us as we learn to invest in others. Jesus the Word-Creator evokes a unique image that takes us back to Genesis where God spoke "let there be" and there it all was. God didn't just speak; He embodied the Word. He literally called creation into being, speaking breath and life into dust that came alive in His image.

My eight year old daughter is a natural writer, and always surprising me with her ever-creative characters and plots. Recently as I was studying about God as Word, I asked her to imagine that as she told her stories, everything that she spoke came to life. Every princess, dragon, and scenic location.

How crazy would it be to imagine something and watch it materialize as you shared your story with others? Perhaps it would be a bit frightening in a Jumanji kind of way, with violent creatures and strange flora emerging from nowhere. What an overwhelming, weighty gift!

Yet this is what Jesus did as Word- He spoke a world into being. In fact, He didn't just talk life into us, the Bible says he sustains all things through His powerful word. (Hebrews 1:1-3) God spoke a story and it happened and only in Him does our story hold together. This is yet another reminder that everything we are belongs to God and all our glory is all ultimately His!

Over and over God calls and uses the weak, lowly, and broken to accomplish His purposes. God designed us for His good works, and He equips us for what He calls us for. In other words, He's already written us powerfully into His redemptive story. As we rest in His presence, He continues to make us Holy and speak His wonderful plans into existence in us.

What does this mean for us as reflective moons? Last I checked I couldn't even speak a coffee into existence. (Although that would be a fantastic super-power.)

Maybe we can't run around speaking our own mini worlds into being. That sounds dangerous. But God has endowed our words with a creative power like His own.

Jesus said, "For the mouth speaks what the heart is full of. A good man brings good things out of the good stored up in him, and an evil man brings evil things out of the evil stored up in him. But I tell you that everyone will have to give account on the day of judgment for every empty word they have spoken."

God can use our speech for powerful good. But our words, apart from God's heart, can bring about more evil. In fact, we'll be called to account not just for evil words but for every "empty word" we speak. An empty word is one without life, hope, or substance. Like an empty picnic basket, it doesn't nourish, replenish, or build anyone up. It's basically a wasted word, dropped without adding value or serving those around us.

But a "full" word contains promise and hope. It builds others up, gently corrects, affirms and blesses. A full word spoken in love has God-given power to lift others into the calling God has for them.

## SPEAK AND INVEST LIFE

In order to invest in others as word-creators we first have to see every single person as an equal reflector. Every person you encounter has God-given worth. Each human is loved and capable of reflecting God regardless of their age, race, gender, physical abilities, past, present, or any other label you might find for them. Our own journey to shine begins in knowing our worth and identity in Christ; likewise, our journey to serve others flows from recognizing them as worthy image-bearers of God.

Only then can we begin the adventure of helping people uncover the fullest potential that God has for them. Sometimes it's as simple as seeing a gift, spark, or passion in someone before they see it in themselves. Someone can't pursue a dream or calling if they don't recognize their gift. So when we speak encouragement and insight, we offer others the courage to envision new dreams, and run with passion the race God has marked for them.

This is leadership in its purest form: to find gifts in others and equip them to run free in those abilities. In doing so, a brother or sister is edified, God receives more glory through their obedience, and we share in that glory as life-speakers. That's relational glory!

Many people have spoken a word into my life that helped me step into God's plan for me. Some friends from church used to meet every week to pray, eat, and challenge each other to follow Christ fully. One week we took turns affirming gifts that we saw in each other, an experiment I highly recommend.

A few people commented on how they admired my ability to waltz up to new people and start conversations, as though that were as crazy as pole-vaulting across the Atlantic Ocean. I didn't realize that for many, talking to strangers actually does feel that crazy. Suddenly I had a fresh view of how my extroverted, people-engaging personality might be part of God's larger purpose for my life.

Likewise, your personality lends itself to your unique purpose. I've seen people who can play host or hostess with ease and make people feel completely at home. It's an amazing gift, but they may not know because it comes so naturally to them. There are others who have blown me away by their ability to coordinate and lead others to accomplish tasks. I'm a dreamer, not an organizer, and I'm in awe of those people. My quiet husband has remarkable insight, and his words carry more weight for his brevity. Brief and quiet are hardly in my vocabulary, but when my husband speaks, people lean in to listen.

Look around, scratch just below the surface, and you'll find a gift in someone else that they haven't unearthed yet. It's actually a lot of fun. We can become gift treasure-hunters seeking ways to build up and invest in friends, neighbors, children, colleagues, church leaders and more. We can build someone up through an encouraging email, conversation, or compliment.

The goal isn't to invent things that a person might be good at. At age six, I briefly took gymnastics classes where most of the girls could do a split as though it were as natural as breathing. I can still picture myself awkwardly coaxing my legs to stretch just a bit more and feeling hot with embarrassment when my best "split" was a foot off the ground. You'd have to break my legs to get them into the correct position. Gymnastics was fun, but it wasn't my gift and my parents would have been foolish to cheer me towards Olympic training.

Sometimes we don't want to hurt people's feelings so we try to affirm what they want to hear. But inflating someone's sense of a gift they don't have can be another way to give an empty word. Other times, someone has a raw gift, but they need improvement in that area. By recognizing the places they're doing well and giving constructive suggestions for where they can grow in their gift, you challenge your brother or sister to reflect more of God's glory.

But always remember, even in constructive feedback, you're seeking to give a "full word." It isn't your job to micromanage or play God in determining someone's gift. We don't need to force someone into what we think their gift is or become a negative voice in their life. Maybe God's doing a new thing in someone that we can't see yet, and we don't want to steamroll that. A good rule of thumb is to make sure whoever we're investing in knows without a doubt that God designed them for good plans, and to never stop seeking His heart.

If you're not sure where to start encouraging someone, pray over a Bible verse with which to encourage them. God's word never returns void, so when we speak His truth into others, we know there's creative power at work. At its core, investing in others means speaking life.

We can also invest in others simply by choosing them. Calling someone out and asking them to join us speaks a powerful word that they are seen and valuable. It reminds them of the dignity that's inherently theirs and invites them to believe that who they are matters. I'm sure you can think of times in your life when someone complimented you, encouraged you, or chose you. Remember the surge of confidence it gave you, the passion it ignited, or the pit it pulled you out of.

Recently at *reNew* Writer's Retreat[1] I found myself taking pictures of attendees and conference leaders who were posing with whimsical props. I'd gotten a few pictures of myself with new friends, and was glad to help capture some memories for others. But I was a bit surprised when one of the main conference leaders called me out and said she'd like to get a picture with me.

Did she really want a picture with a self-published, stay-at-home mom when there were so many brighter attendees present? In the simple gesture of choosing to take a picture with me, this woman called me to see myself as her peer, as a writer, and as someone worth being with. It may sound silly, but the simple act of choosing someone is powerful.

Many of us can think of the opposite as well: a time when someone excluded us or made us feel "less than." I cringe as I recall doing that to a good friend once.

I'd been asked to join a group that my friend didn't get an invite to. She'd been longing for such a group and was understandably upset that I didn't reach out to include her. Instead of asking her to join, I came up with all my perfectly valid reasons why it was OK for me to be in a group without her. The bottom line: I hurt a good friend in the process of trying to protect my own worth.

Needing to validate ourselves is never a good reason to be exclusive. Whenever possible, we should ask how we can include others to foster belonging, diversity, and passion. Inclusion acknowledges the dignity in others and invites them to stand confidently in their value. It breaks the power of pride, envy and selfish ambition.

One way to combine both speaking life and inclusion is to make a long-term investment in someone through mentoring, shepherding, or parenting. Viewing mentoring and parenting as a chance to invest God's glory in the next generation changes the way we view even the mundane tasks we face.

We're not just meeting for coffee, asking questions or listening to someone share their day to day journeys; we're helping to build someone towards their full potential. Likewise, we're not just changing diapers, chauffeuring kids, or arbitrating disputes; we're helping kids see their God-given worth as He writes something beautiful through their lives.

God invested in us so we could invest in others. If you're looking for a place to start, I'd suggest you make a list of people you regularly encounter in your life at school, home, church, work or other social groups. Who might you already be building into? Who might need a little extra mentoring or encouragement? Ask God how you can help someone else reflect Him.

## WHEN GLORY-SHARING FEELS LIKE LESS PIE FOR YOU

I can't talk about all the rosy aspects of glory-sharing without addressing that massive elephant off in the corner of the room. It's one thing to believe in and cheer for relational glory. Woohoo! It's awesome to invest in and encourage others to be all that God called them to be. High fives all around!

But we all know that sometimes truly encouraging others to step into who they're made to be requires us to sacrifice. It involves us giving up a glory that we felt we had the right to in order to make room for someone else to step up and reflect God. Or it requires us to give control of something to another person who could make us look bad or who might not do things just the way we'd have done them.

More than one person took a giant risk in letting me speak in front of my church the first time. For one, they gave up a position that could have gone to someone more qualified, or that they could have filled themselves. They took the chance that I'd totally bomb and accidentally say something theologically unsound, or mispronounce one of those Old Testament names (like Mahershalalhashbaz) or worse. But because they let me speak not once but several times over the last couple years, they've allowed God to help me see and develop a still-growing gift.

If we truly believe God has gifted someone, we'll be willing to back up our words by giving them a place or platform to use their gift if it's in our ability. The more we do this, the less tightly we hold onto our own glory, and the more God's glory spreads. It's a win-win, but it sometimes feels like a loss to us.

Last year I started an experiment called "Friend Post Fridays" where I find guests to post on my blog once a month. I may not have a lucrative platform to offer someone, but I have a microphone and decided to share it. I've been so encouraged and joyful in hearing other stories and seeing how they connect with readers. But at the same time, there have been moments when guest posters got more shares, more likes, more apparent glory than my own posts. What gives?

It's times like these that we can feel that investing in others actually diminished our own glory. This takes us right back to the world's lies that the glory-pie is finite and the one with the most glory wins the most worth. We have to staunchly remind ourselves that our worth is pre-secure, God's glory will never run out, and giving up ourselves for God's kingdom has far more value than we realize.

When Jesus walked the earth, He was undoubtedly the most qualified person alive to do all the healing, teaching, and baptizing. He could have told His disciples to sit back while He did all the kingdom work Himself so that people knew without a doubt that the credit belonged to Him. He had better reason than any of us to focus on His platform and follower count.

But instead, what did Jesus do? He invited the disciples into the miracles He did. He asked them to feed 5,000 people on a remote hill (Matthew 14:16); He sent them out "gave them authority to drive out impure spirits and to heal every disease and sickness." (Matthew 10:1)

In fact, despite all the amazing things Jesus was doing, He told His disciples that His death was a bonus for them because then His Spirit would come and fill them in a fresh way. Jesus made this audacious claim: "'...whoever believes in me will do the works I have been doing, and they will do even greater things than these, because I am going to the Father.'" (John 14:12) Jesus shows us that the greatest way to grow His kingdom is to always be giving authority and opportunities to others.

Pushing our way to the front and hogging glory that was never ours to possess actually leaves us empty at the end. It stunts the kingdom. But God uses our letting go to multiply His kingdom like we could never imagine. Trying to hold onto our glory cuts off the very source of our passion and gifts, debilitating others and ourselves. But the other option- giving up- frees and spreads glory like oxygen to fire.

Where do you have the ability to use your talent to teach or invest in others? What platform or role do you currently have that could be loaned to someone else to help them grow in their own gifts and reflection of God? Be a moon that leads other moons to the Light.

# MOON UNIVERSITY
## Lesson Seven

**Star Lie #7**: If we invest in someone else, there will be less value left for us.

**Moon Truth #7**: God designed us to magnify glory in relationship with others.

Question 1: Aside from the example in this chapter, can you think of other ways that God magnifies glory within Himself or through us? Why do you think God isn't afraid to share glory?

Question 2: Can you think of an example of someone in your life who gave you a "full word" and encouraged you to walk in God's heart for you? What did that feel like and where did it lead you?

Question 3: Has someone excluded or discouraged you and stomped out a passion or dream? How can you let God speak truth into that dream again? What does He say about you?

Question 4: Maybe you are an encourager on steroids, or maybe you're someone who just needs to focus on building up one person at a time right now. That's OK. Either way, who is one person this week you can intentionally speak a full word to or encourage in their gift this week?

Question 5: Is there something you're afraid to let go of even though you know it would encourage or help somebody else?

Question 6: Have you ever considered that you can't shine unless God invests shine in you? Spend a few minutes contemplating His incredible glory. Worship Him for who He is. Thank Him for all the ways He pours His own goodness and grace into your life.

# 8
# GIFTS: THE GOOD, THE BAD, AND THE UGLY

"The God who made the world and everything in it is the Lord of heaven and earth and does not live in temples built by human hands. And he is not served by human hands, as if he needed anything. Rather, he himself gives everyone life and breath and everything else."
**-Acts 17:24-25**

## THE IDOLATRY OF GIFTS

In first grade there was an obnoxious, teacher's pet in my class that thrived on being one of the smartest. She once corrected the teacher and got a sticker for it, which she proudly showed off to her classmates. (I mean, get over yourself already.)

The teacher raved about her reading at a fifth grade level, which put her in a whole separate color category of reading than other kids in class (because apparently our academic abilities need to be color-coded). She was gifted, but obviously her gift had become all about herself and her own proud identity.

I should know because...wait for it...I was that obnoxious first grader. (Feel free to judge my six year old self.)

Yes, I was one of those kids who did really well in school. Somehow I knew at even a young age that I had an ability that didn't come naturally to just everyone. Other people might be the funniest, the best at soccer, or the most natural at making friends. Being the smartest was a sturdy shelf on which to place my worth.

The problem was that my gift quickly became my identity. To me, having a gift meant I was set apart from others, that I mattered uniquely, that I owned something others didn't. My ability was for me and about me. I didn't think of my talent as a unique way to serve others, but as a unique way to shine and matter.

I now have a third grade daughter who reminds me so much of my smarty-pants self at her age. I'm thankful that school comes easily to her and that she's excelling academically. I'd have to be unconscious not to be proud of her.

When she comes home from school I don't chide her for her brains or stare at her sternly while forcing her to write "being smart is not my identity" one hundred times on the back of her homework papers. But I'm trying to teach my kids early on that the gifts they have are tools not labels.

I'd rather my daughter be in tune to the needs of those around her than be a straight-A student. I'd rather she be passionate about changing lives than read above grade level. I'd rather her fail at all the places the world says are important and live freely as a moon chasing God. He has given my girl an amazingly tender heart, which I pray will inform how she uses the knowledge in her head. I pray she'll know that her identity is a loved child of God. Period.

My daughter's gifts are good, and so are yours. They're part of our reflectional DNA. But, perhaps especially in the church, they can become an unhealthy focus without being grounded in the God who loves us regardless of gifts. In the church, in addition to our talents and natural aptitudes, we talk about spiritual gifts. If natural gifts make us feel valuable, how much more the thought that we've been given gifts of the Holy Spirit for the purpose of God's kingdom.

Passages like 1 Corinthians 12 offer us lists of possible gifts that each of us might be endowed with by God's Spirit: wisdom, prophecy, teaching, healing, guidance and helping, speaking in tongues, and discernment to name a few.

I'm not going to give you a quiz today to help you pinpoint your exact spiritual or physical giftedness. There are many other books and websites that can give you greater clarity for your gifts or personality. If you're unsure of your passion, a quick internet search of "spiritual gifts assessment" or "personality assessment" (such as Myers Briggs[1]) might be a valuable tool for you. I've found clarity in my life through better understanding my personality and inherent gifts.

But before you define your niche, you need to know your niche doesn't define you. Know yourself, believe that God has put special purposes over your life, and walk boldly in your gifts. But our bottom line identity is a child of God. Nothing more, nothing less. When we lose sight of our intrinsic worth in God, we begin to twist even God-given things in our pursuit of significance. Sometimes we slap spiritual labels right over our God-given name, and forget who we truly are.

This labeling can send us right back to the trap of comparison which, like water to a sponge, quickly fills every pore of our lives. We subconsciously find ourselves ranking the gifts of the Spirit, wondering if perhaps God really didn't create all gifts equally. Maybe teaching is a little higher than wisdom, we muse, but helping sounds like no fun so that's probably a bottom-of-the-barrel, entry-level gift.

*Dear God let someone else be a helper, I really want the gift of healing because that seems pretty useful and profound (which, conveniently, would make me useful and profound!)*

We measure ourselves by "more" or "less" but ironically never "enough." Yet God says you are. When gifts cause us to be possessive, we hold them tightly instead of viewing them as tools to free others with. These gifts are pieces of God on loan to us, and they're made for giving back.

First Corinthians 12:4-7 says, "There are different kinds of gifts, but the same Spirit distributes them. There are different kinds of service, but the same Lord. There are different kinds of working, but in all of them and in everyone it is the same God at work. Now to each one the manifestation of the Spirit is given for the common good."

Our gifts are made for the good of community. God's gifts aren't short-sighted or meant to boost our self-esteem: they're part of His grand narrative, made for His kingdom and His glory. But the minute we treat our gifts like name-brand clothing labels, they become an idol that distracts us from God's heart.

## GOD'S HEART IN OUR DIFFERENCES

One of the most important lessons we can learn as a moon is that every moon shines the very same light. I realize that my moon analogy breaks down a little bit at this point because, last I checked, we only have one moon. (My active imagination is now picturing our earth's chaotic state if billions of moons were orbiting like crazed lunar bumper cars. Where were we again...?)

But imagine that each of us is a moon, suspended in our galaxy, facing Jesus; no matter how big or small, bumpy or round, we share a common Light Source. This means that regardless of our gifts, our talents, our mistakes, our platform or age, each of us equally borrows our light.

So that person who's on the stage all the time, teaching or singing in the spotlight? She is no more valuable than the person who serves coffee in the lobby or cleans after everyone has gone. The time spent serving and loving people outside the church walls is just as significant as the time pastors pour into their ministry. There are no shinier jobs in the kingdom, because we all reflect the same God in our gifts.

God, in His beauty, uses each of our unique reflections of Him to own and respond to a different part of His heart and passion. This is a very good thing because God's heart for justice and redemption spans far wider than we could imagine. While all of us are called to love God and others and break chains of injustice in the world, none of us is individually equipped for the magnitude of that task.

Although we're equal reflectors, our missions in life should not look the same. God reflects off each one differently to accomplish His larger purpose. He clearly has a heart for the vulnerable, but we aren't all called to adopt. We aren't all called to prison ministry. We aren't all called to care for struggling teen moms. We won't all become animal rights activists or environmental lawyers.

Sometimes our differences cause us to judge instead of embrace. We can become so passionate about the things God has uniquely put on our hearts that we begin to assume those are the things He cares about the most. We might assume our passion is more noble or more godly than another person's.

We cannot mistake our God-given passion for God's single priority.

At times our passions overlap and we join forces with others to change the world through His love. Sometimes our passions differ and we can trust that God is using those differences to fully reflect His heart in all aspects of the world.

We can spend our time criticizing or pointing fingers at those who don't adopt or don't give money to crisis pregnancy centers or whose hearts aren't moved by Sarah McLachlan's pleas to help neglected animals. We can accuse others of falling short of God's plan because their version of church doesn't look like ours.

Or, we can acknowledge that perhaps He has put another piece of His passion in their hearts to run with. This isn't an excuse to ignore our part in the things God cares about because "that's someone else's job." Rather, it's an invitation to see each of our passions as a piece of the larger puzzle of God's heart.

As we humbly realize that God shines on each of us uniquely yet as a whole, we can enjoy who we were made to be and support others in what He's reflecting off of them. This idea also frees us from guilt in comparing ourselves in negative ways to the achievements of others.

If we're each made to reflect Him a little bit differently, we don't need to strive to be what someone else is. We simply need to be who our Father has called us to be and support our brothers and sisters in God's heart for them.

## BUT WHAT IF WE'RE THE SAME?

Though it can be hard for us to accept the fact that God may be working through our differences to accomplish His full purpose, sometimes it's harder for us to work alongside those who are very similar to us. It's like when two women show up as guests to a wedding wearing the same dress. Suddenly we feel a little foolish, less unique, more concerned that someone might be wearing our gift better.

Personally, I love that we're all different in the body of Christ. I love the idea of "different" because it takes me back to my first grader self when I had my own little corner of significance with just my name on it. But it's much harder for me to be around people with similar gifts and abilities because I fear they might squeeze me right out of my seat of significance.

Today my title of choice is "writer" and "speaker" because I come fully alive in those activities. I'm a communicator who thrives on social interactions- both are part of how my DNA reflects God's heart.

If you put me in a room of people with different gifts than mine, I'm happy as a clam. I can mingle with the hospitality team or type-A leaders and fully appreciate their gifts. (No shine overlap there.) But stick me in a room full of bloggers and speakers and my competitive radar goes up. I start looking at how many followers they have or the content of their work. Is it too similar to mine? Why can't all the Christian women be blogging about plumbing or taxidermy or uses for potatoes instead of about faith?

Suddenly I have a fear that if I don't personally own a corner of God's light, then my light is irrelevant. What if I'm simply not good enough or unique enough? What if my reflected light is too similar to be seen? What if I'm not really needed? Gah!

The truth is that each of us can only reflect what God has already created. Since He's the Source of light, there will be times when more than one of us are reflecting His light in similar ways. But it's not our job to shine a light that no one else is shining- that's not possible. It's our job to shine a light period. God wants you to reflect Him to that unique group of people you're surrounded by. Which means God will use other people to influence people you will never encounter.

Call me selfish, but that's crazy hard for me. I want to feel like I have something exclusive to offer the kingdom, but God doesn't give us copyright on any of His material. Wisdom, truth, salvation, abilities, gifts: these all originate with God and He entrusts us as stewards of each one for His purposes.

Recently at a writer's conference, a workshop facilitator quoted author Jefferson Bethke's book *Jesus > Religion*. Guess what his excerpt was about? Reflecting God like the moon. If I knew how to insert a fuming emoji here, I would, but speaking emoji isn't my spiritual gift.

Instead of enjoying that wonderful excerpt I was actually annoyed that someone got the idea out before I did. I was discouraged because I thought my idea was original enough to earn me some value points.

But then God reminded me that maybe seeing a God idea show up in someone else is actually confirmation that it is His idea. Surely if He has universal wisdom to share He will repeat His same message through multiple people in a variety of ways. God can use me uniquely with a message or gift that is redundant because God's Word doesn't change. He's the same yesterday, today, and tomorrow, and yet He wants to recycle His wisdom through you for just such a time as this, for just such a place.

In case you haven't noticed, the internet is kind of a big deal lately and growing every second. Overlapping ideas will occur more frequently because we're connected to a multitude of people with similar wisdom, platforms and gifts as ours. More and more we'll confront the truth of Ecclesiastes 1:9: "there is nothing new under the sun."

We can let that thought send us into our old star-panic, or we can walk free in this concept by acknowledging that God owns all these ideas. Every good and perfect gift is from God, and in His vast generosity He's allowed us to be ambassadors of His gifts, His ideas, His gospel, to the world. The world isn't changed by a copywritten gospel with patented ideas, it's transformed by God's love and truth that has no limits and needs no permission to be shared.

In his book, Tribes, Seth Godin calls us out on the silliness of trying to validate ourselves by taking credit for ideas. He says, "There's no record of Martin Luther King, Jr., or Gandhi whining about credit. Credit isn't the point. Change is.²" Ouch. That cuts straight to my pride.

Philippians 1:15-18 puts it this way, "It is true that some preach Christ out of envy and rivalry, but others out of goodwill. The latter do so out of love, knowing that I am put here for the defense of the gospel. The former preach Christ out of selfish ambition, not sincerely, supposing that they can stir up trouble for me while I am in chains. But what does it matter? The important thing is that in every way, whether from false motives or true, Christ is preached. And because of this I rejoice."

Paul reiterates Christ's heart: credit isn't the point. Having an original idea isn't the point. Finding out completely unique ways to shine God's light like no one else isn't the point. The point is that in all things Christ Himself, our Light, is spread deep into every crack of a dark world. That means I can rejoice whether His truth shines off me or someone else.

Yes, God wants to use you uniquely. After all, you yourself are His handiwork, and He has designed you and prepared you for good works. But you were made to point others to Him, not yourself. Stars need credit for shining to matter, but a moon is excited whenever its Source is reflected...even by other moons.

## REFLECTING HIS STRENGTHS IN OUR WEAKNESS

Have you ever boasted in your weaknesses? It's not a popular activity. I like thinking about how God is working through the gifts and abilities that He's given me. Go ahead, God, shine off my visible good spots! (And thanks for those, by the way.)

If you're like me, you'd prefer not to let your weaknesses hang out on the clothesline like dirty unmentionables for the world to see. Oh I'm not so concerned about surface weaknesses: you know, the way I'm so ridiculously disorganized (bless my heart), my endearing weakness for all things java, or my tendency towards whimsical awkwardness. Can God shine off those weaknesses? Sure, why not? He's awfully bright, you know.

But in Second Corinthians, Paul throws a curveball at me by bringing up a much deeper weakness. Paul says, "Therefore, in order to keep me from becoming conceited, I was given a thorn in my flesh, a messenger of Satan, to torment me. Three times I pleaded with the Lord to take it away from me."

The man is painfully vague about what this "thorn" was, but he's crystal clear about this: God didn't take his weakness away. Instead God says, "'My grace is sufficient for you, for my power is made perfect in weakness.'" (2 Corinthians 12:9-10)

So what does Paul logically conclude? Does he cry out to God that this weakness is keeping Him from fully serving God? (I've told God that before.) Does he kick the dust and accuse God of abandoning Him? (I've also done that.) Does he conclude that he can't possibly reflect God with such a glaring weakness? (Ok, if you haven't figured it out yet, these are all my thoughts, not Paul's.)

No, instead Paul declares: "I will boast all the more gladly about my weaknesses, so that Christ's power may rest on me. That is why, for Christ's sake, I delight in weaknesses, in insults, in hardships, in persecutions, in difficulties. For when I am weak, then I am strong."

I don't think Paul is talking about a "cute" weakness here. I doubt Paul was asking God to take away his finger-nail biting habit, or his propensity to snort when he laughed. I'm pretty sure it was worse than poor grammar or an inability to ever show up to a coffee date with the other apostles on time.

Paul is talking about a serious, persistent weakness. He doesn't strike me as a reserved guy, but he didn't really care to broadcast the specifics of this weakness live. It was a painful, regular part of his life that he wished to get rid of. But Paul allowed God to plant a fundamental truth in his heart that actually turned his brokenness into show-stopping cause for celebration.

Far from preventing us from shining, God intentionally created our weaknesses to reflect Him in ways that our strengths never could. Our weaknesses, in God's hands, are some of our greatest assets. Maybe we need to rethink weakness and let Him rewrite our resumes.

## WHEN GOD WRITES YOUR RESUME

Confession: sometimes when I go to a conference and read the bios for the speakers, or even read the author bio on the back of a book, I get obnoxiously critical. It's like everyone and their mother has these legendary, demi-god like accomplishments that the rest of us normal humans can't reach.

They graduated from the top of their class at Harvard and went on to get a master's degree in something that I don't have enough education to pronounce, or perhaps they survived a tragedy in their home-country and went on to lead a non-violent revolution that saved millions. Maybe they've got three New York Times bestselling books that they wrote in their spare time while running multiple humanitarian relief organizations and backpacking across Europe.

Some people seem to have strengths oozing out of their pores. When we introduce ourselves to others, we logically advertise our strengths, because we believe they make us valuable and worth listening to.

People don't start bios by talking about their addictions or problems, unless they've overcome them. People don't shake your hand for the first time and launch into a list of their habitual sins. I've never seen a bio that highlighted anyone's incompetence, foolishness, lack of education, or inabilities.

Yet, if we truly want to shine we should take a close look at what Paul said in the passage above. It's not that our weaknesses in and of themselves are these bright objects of beauty. But it's in our weakness that we realize our utter dependence on God and His light.

In the areas of our lives where we have no control, God has the power to show up as only He can. It's in our lack that He is able to supply His glory instead of whatever glow-stick strengths we think we have to boast about.

As weakness grows our dependence on God, it shrinks our tendency to become conceited. In our strengths we can easily become convinced that we're responsible for the light that God is shining off of us. At least a little. I mean, after all...check out our good Christian resumes. But Paul reminds us that we play by the rules of God's kingdom.

"Brothers and sisters, think of what you were when you were called. Not many of you were wise by human standards; not many were influential; not many were of noble birth. But God chose the *foolish* things of the world to shame the wise; God chose the *weak* things of the world to shame the strong. God chose the *lowly* things of this world and the *despised* things—and the things *that are not*—to nullify the things that are, so that no one may boast before him. It is because of him that you are in Christ Jesus, who has become for us wisdom from God—that is, our righteousness, holiness and redemption. Therefore, as it is written: 'Let the one who boasts boast in the Lord.'" (1 Corinthians 1:26-31, emphasis mine)

Paul says, "Look at you! Most of you didn't graduate from Harvard. The majority of you weren't voted most likely to succeed. You didn't have influence or come from prestigious families. You're not Hollywood stars or big-name church people- you're just regular Joes and Janes. And that's exactly the way God planned it."

God actually picked the lesser things in the eyes of the world to brightly burn his own righteousness into. He isn't waiting for the brightest of the bright and creamiest of the crop to work for Him.

God is unapologetically delighted to use our washed up, embarrassing weakness to call attention to His own vast strength. He sees our frame, knows we are dust, holds us together and gives us our very being. Like a coach who sees potential in his underdog team, God wants us to give Him our weakness so He can turn it into a glory nobody saw coming- a glory that is so beyond our ability that we don't even try to take credit for it.

Owning our weakness also reminds those around us that it's OK to have imperfect craters and blemishes. God speaks a poetry through our weakness that our strengths never could. In fact, our strengths reach farther when people realize our humanness as well. Broken and imperfect people need to know we're broken and imperfect too.

## CIRCUMSTANCES: THE GIFT NOBODY WANTS

Recently a friend at church ran a family prayer night for Advent, and brought a beautifully wrapped present as an object lesson for the kids. She lured the children in by describing the gift as a useful item that their parents bought all the time. She scanned the room and called on my daughter who skipped up to the stage and excitedly opened...a roll of toilet paper. (My friend threw in a Starbucks gift card as well so as not to seem cruel, and now my daughter has been ruined by the taste of blended ice coffee.)

The toilet paper represented something we truly need but don't necessarily want. Nobody wakes up Christmas morning with visions of two-ply dancing in their heads. (Although, honestly, when was the last time you craved sugar plums either?) Yet we wouldn't get very far in our day without some ever practical TP. Likewise, there are many gifts we've been given by God that are very useful but don't necessarily feel so gifty.

Just like weakness, we don't always consider that God uses the unique circumstances in our lives as an amazing gift we can give to others. Everything that's happened to us is part of the story that helps us connect with those around us.

And the crazier part is, typically the circumstances in our lives that are the most difficult are the parts of our lives people most need to hear. Maybe you've lived through the heartbreak of divorce, struggled as a single parent, experienced trauma or abuse as a child. Perhaps you've moved so many times you don't know where home is, or you've lost a baby to miscarriage. Maybe you've got a chronic medical condition or mental illness. Maybe you made some horrible choices or maybe you reacted to the terrible choices of others.

None of those things feels very gift-like. That's unimaginably worse than opening toilet paper for Christmas. I'm not saying that God is the originator of your pain, or that His idea of a perfect world included suffering. But God is so much stronger than any evil, that He weaves some of His best redemptive stories through our broken ones.

If you look closely at ministries, organizations, and movements that are changing the world, you'll likely find a common thread: they were birthed out of difficult experiences.

Christine Cain turned her painful backstory into the A21 organization that protects others from abuse.[3] Carol Kent allowed God to turn her son's agonizing story of incarceration into a message of hope, and her son's negative circumstance became his ministry opportunity.[4] Nelson Mandela harnessed imprisonment and suffering to create equality and spark a movement of justice. The difficulty of pregnancy with diabetes was a catalyst for me to pursue adoption. What is your pain producing?

Second Corinthians 1:3-5 says,

"Praise be to the God and Father of our Lord Jesus Christ, the Father of compassion and the God of all comfort, who comforts us in all our troubles, so that we can comfort those in any trouble with the comfort we ourselves receive from God. For just as we share abundantly in the sufferings of Christ, so also our comfort abounds through Christ."

I admit I have a love-hate relationship with this passage. Part of me wants to say, "Really God? You mean to tell me all the crap I go through is so that I can comfort someone ELSE going through suffering? Why not just eliminate all the suffering and call it a day?"

But the verse also reminds me that I follow a Christ who suffered for me. For us. He's close to the brokenhearted, intimate with our pain because He walked it. Our God chose to suffer to be near us, and ultimately to be our comfort. The sobering reality is that reflecting God means that we will share in Christ's suffering. Yet through that suffering, Christ allows us to reflect His deep love and comfort.

I can speak all day about my strengths, my bright spots, my success, my wins. But people are far more ready to listen when they know my struggles, past and present, and the altogether human journey I've walked.

What of your circumstances feels more like a ball and chain than a gift of freedom? May we trust that God can use those exact circumstances to reflect Him most profoundly. May He use every part of our lives to lead us to those who need to know the hope we've found in the Light. Because that's when the tide begins to turn.

# MOON UNIVERSITY
## Lesson Eight

**Star Lie #8**: Our gifts are our most powerful tools to reflect God.

**Moon Truth #8**: God is powerfully reflected through every surrendered area of our lives.

Question 1: Where have you tried to define yourself by your gifts or roles in life? Have they become idols? How does viewing yourself as a child of God, above all else, help you live like a moon?

Question 2: Have you ever mistaken the passion God has put on your heart for God's top priority? Or have you thought your passion was less important than someone else's? How has that comparison affected you and your ability to work with others for the common good?

Question 3: "The world isn't changed by a copywritten gospel with patented ideas, it's transformed by God's love and truth that has no limits and needs no permission to be shared." (pg. 82)
How does holding on to our own glory keep us from changing the world?

Question 4: Do you struggle more with wishing you had gifts like someone else or with constantly comparing yourself to those with similar gifts? How does viewing us all as reflectors of the same light help you to rest securely in who God made you?

Question 5: Have you ever viewed your weakness or suffering as a gift? Looking at your own life, can you see ways God has used those difficulties in your life to change you? To change others?

# 9
# TURNING THE TIDE

"For he has rescued us from the dominion of darkness and brought us into the kingdom of the Son he loves."
**-Colossians 3:9**

"Let us not become weary in doing good, for at the proper time we will reap a harvest if we do not give up."
   **-Galatians 6:9**

## OUR GIFTS ARE MADE TO INVEST

Once we realize the truth about gifts and the pitfalls of striving to be bright for the world to see, we may begin a misguided mass reevaluation of our lives in an attempt to purge our previous light seeking. Suddenly we see pride danger signs everywhere and we become suspicious that any public action is a false-glory trap.

*"You want me to do announcements on stage? Can I do them from the back of the auditorium? I really just don't need the spotlight." "Ew, why would you compliment me for my business skills? Be gone, you pride trap!" "You're actually asking me to lead a group of people? Um, no. I see what you're doing, and I prefer to decline opportunities for conceit to develop unnecessarily in my life."*

In our diligence to avoid shining for the wrong reasons, we can unwittingly fall into an entirely different pot-hole: false humility. This is yet another distorted truth that the enemy would love us to believe: that shining at all is a prideful attempt to steal God's glory.

Once again, it helps to think about the moon. Have you ever heard someone comment about how the moon is such a prideful jerk? Or have you heard someone say they can't stand the way the moon has the gall to steal the sun's light? No. We enjoy and appreciate the beauty of the moon, knowing its luminescence isn't stolen but given. The moon is simply being the reflective surface it was made to be, without strife or fear of being glorious.

The same is true with us. We acknowledge that God is the giver of our circumstances, our abilities and passions. That is our unique moon-ness. Shining in God's gifts and timing is hardly an act of pride, but the purest form of humility and worship.

We say to God, *"You've made me and who I am, and your light alone can make me shine. Shine your everything so brightly against my nothing that others see more of You."*

If you're still skeptical about whether it's OK to be seen or to sparkle and still honor God, let me ease your mind with a fictional story, or parable, that Jesus used to teach his followers.

This vignette begins with a man of means who is just about to leave for an extended trip. He wants to put his assets to work, but he can't take care of financial investments himself while he's traveling. Instead, the man entrusts various amounts of his money to three servants: to one he gives five bags of gold, to one two bags, and to still another one bag. Though they've received different amounts, he expects each one to show a return on his money when he comes home.

After his trip, he finds that the first two servants have invested their original gold. Jesus doesn't tell us how, (the story isn't about how Jesus would tackle Wall Street) but both of these servants double the amount of gold their master entrusted them with. With joy, he calls them "good and faithful servant[s]." (Matthew 25:23) However, the last servant with only one bag of gold has a sobering, different story:

"Then the man who had received one bag of gold came. 'Master,' he said, 'I knew that you are a hard man, harvesting where you have not sown and gathering where you have not scattered seed. So I was afraid and went out and hid your gold in the ground. See, here is what belongs to you.' "His master replied, 'You wicked, lazy servant! So you knew that I harvest where I have not sown and gather where I have not scattered seed? Well then, you should have put my money on deposit with the bankers, so that when I returned I would have received it back with interest.'" (Matthew 25:24-27)

The master represents God, and each of us is one of His servants. The bags of gold represent not just physical resources, but also the gifts, abilities, and circumstances God has put in each of our lives. God says to us: "From everyone who has been given much, much will be demanded;

and from the one who has been entrusted with much, much more will be asked." (Luke 12:48) God has given you exactly who you are, yet it's all His "money" if you will, entrusted to you for a time.

For whatever reason, despite the dozens of times I've heard this story, I suddenly read it with fresh eyes and saw myself differently. God was speaking to me that a fear of shining or using borrowed gifts isn't actually humility; it's hiding what was never mine to hide.

The master calls the servant wicked and lazy, which might sound harsh. But the strong language is a reminder that when God invests glory in us and we cover it up in fear or complacency, we're actually dishonoring God. We can't hide what isn't ours to hide.

Let me put it this way: Should Lebron James reel in his basketball talent on the court to take the edge off his shine? Should the late Billy Graham have limited his crusades to only very small audiences to avoid too much glory-reflection? Should the girl who leads worship at your church throw in a botched note here and there lest she over-sparkle in front of everyone?

Should you turn down every promotion at work to avoid standing out as management? Should Rob Morris never have helped start Love146 in case he got some extra media attention? Should I avoid publishing a book because it might take off and make me look good?

I think we can safely say that using our gifts isn't the problem- it's our attitude, our posture before God. Being good at something, and even being seen while using our gifts, are not wrong. True humility is a constant process of acknowledging what we've been given and learning to lay that glory down instead of grasping at it for ourselves.

As we run our race well, we inspire others to run too. In the process of writing this book, God has connected me with so many other writers in hiding. Some were afraid to step out and start writing publicly at all; others had an idea for a book that was sitting on a shelf of seemingly impossible dreams in their mind. One person was spurred on to finish the book he started. God always wants to multiply our investment, and He does that partly by motivating others through our steps of faith.

In Hebrews 11, Paul lists several men and women that changed their world through faith. He knew that with each successive story, his audience would begin to visualize their own calling of faith as well. Paul concludes,

"Therefore, since we are surrounded by such a great cloud of witnesses, let us throw off everything that hinders and the sin that so easily entangles. And let us run with perseverance the race marked out for us, fixing our eyes on Jesus, the pioneer and perfecter of faith." (Hebrews 12:1-2)

We were made to run as hard as we can after God, and lead others by example.

I believe God is saying to each of us, *"Come and dance with me and let me show you what I've made you for, how I've uniquely created you to reflect My light.*

*Breathe my gifts in and out again, always out again. Keep your eyes fixed on me, and you'll find I'm actually multiplying MY glory through you. Eyes on me, give and take, hold nothing tightly and you have no need to fear shining brightly."*

Don't shrink back from all God has for you. Humility isn't hiding from the light, but acknowledging our Light Source as we stand full in His glory.

## FOR SUCH A TIME AS THIS

There's a story in the Bible about a woman named Esther who, if she were in the parable above, barely started with a full bag of gold at all. For starters, she was an orphan, raised only by her faithful Uncle Mordecai. But beyond her lost family roots, she lived among a rootless race.

Her people, the Jews, had been conquered and exiled from their land and were now ruled by the fiery-tempered, Persian king, Xerxes. He wasn't someone you'd even want to have dinner with, but with Esther's luck, that's just what happened.

One day the king had a major spat with his queen and decided to pick a new one, beauty pageant style. In our culture, being selected for a nation-wide beauty competition might sound like an amazing opportunity for stardom. But this wasn't quite like *The Bachelor*. Esther didn't have a choice to sign up and her two possible outcomes were marrying Mr. Less-Than-Stable, or ending up as a discarded leftover in his harem of concubines (not the most romantic of options).

She was herded together with who knows how many other beautiful young women, away from all she'd known, and made to undergo long-term beauty treatments as preparation to stand before the king. Did she lose part of her identity as her yearlong makeover progressed? Did she long for the comforting conversation of her uncle? Was she terrified of being picked, or numb at the thought of what rejection would mean? Did she feel used, like just another pretty number?

Regardless of how she felt, she wasn't just a number to God. He had a story pre-written for her, a glorious plan beneath the surface of her pain. As frightening as it may have been, the king chose her for his new bride. Overnight, Esther went from unknown orphan to queen of her land. It sounds like so many rags to riches star stories we secretly hope will happen to us. Yet in that precarious place of influence, she was about to face her worst fear yet.

Just after Esther was made queen, the king elevated a man named Haman to an extremely prominent position in the palace. But unlike Esther, Haman's life goal was to achieve more power and honor. Haman's new promotion came with a sweet perk: all the royal officials had to kneel for him when he walked by. That's even better than having a reserved parking space at your office.

But one day, Haman found out that Mordecai was refusing to bow to him. (He still didn't know Mordecai was Esther's uncle.) Haman's head had gotten so big, that he may have slightly over-reacted to Mordecai's insolence.

Esther 3:5-6 says, "When Haman saw that Mordecai would not kneel down or pay him honor, he was enraged. Yet having learned who Mordecai's people were, he scorned the idea of killing only Mordecai. Instead Haman looked for a way to destroy all Mordecai's people, the Jews, throughout the whole kingdom of Xerxes."

Talk about a plot-twist. Esther had barely gotten used to the idea of a tiara when Mordecai told her the ghastly news: Haman was scheming to annihilate Esther's people. Her uncle followed his earth-shattering announcement with an equally weighty appeal: would she use her position as queen to save the Jewish race?

Esther? The world had been against her since childhood, and now her own race incriminated her. She was supposed to influence the king? She was supposed to approach Mr. Temper-Tantrum (a violation of the law) after he fired his last queen for a teeny act of defiance? Little orphan Esther was supposed to save God's people?

But Mordecai whispered words that reverberate through the generations: "...if you remain silent at this time, relief and deliverance for the Jews will arise from another place, but you and your father's family will perish. And who knows but that you have come to your royal position for such a time as this?" (Esther 4:14)

In other words, she could invest her influence, or bury it. Her choice.

What does her story teach us about God's plan for us as moons? First of all, we should notice that Esther didn't strive to become an influential person. She wasn't loitering outside the castle waiting for an invitation; she wasn't periodically submitting her resume to see if the king was looking to hire an intern to train for the position of future wife. She didn't need to position herself, because God pulled the good, the seemingly bad, and the ugly of her life to bring her precisely to His purpose.

In fact we see this law at work over and over in the people we consider heroes of the Bible. Noah didn't beg God to give Him the task of saving the human race. Abraham didn't seek God out to become a great nation. Mary didn't take a million babysitting courses or "Holy Lamaze" to prove to God she could handle His Son. Saul, later known as Paul, was actually trying to avoid Jesus right before God launched him into one of the most influential ministries of church history.

What did Noah, Abraham, Mary, Paul and Esther all possess? They had faith strong enough to allow them to simply surrender to God's plan. Noah built when he couldn't see a reason yet. Abraham believed God's promise was sturdier than the problem of old age.

Mary said to the angel delivering the life-altering news, "I am the Lord's servant...may your word to me be fulfilled." (Luke 1:38) Paul went from killing followers of Jesus to preaching that same Jesus in the span of a few Bible verses. That's surrendered faith, the mantra of the moon.

And Esther? She asked her uncle to organize a fast for her. Then she replied with one of the most moon-like things I've ever heard: "When this is done, I will go to the king, even though it is against the law. And if I perish, I perish." (Esther 4:16)

In faith she stepped out, surrendering every part of herself (including her life), to God's plan. There was no striving for significance, simply faith in the moment of truth. Yet the result was nothing short of the salvation of her people.

What if we lived as though God had put life or death kingdom purposes in our own lives? What if we lived as though God, apart from our striving and grasping at purpose, was intentionally setting us up to powerfully reflect His light in our generation? What if we lived like God had called each of us to unique influence for such a time as this if only we'd live surrendered to Him in faith?

Because it's true.

I don't care who you are, what your qualifications, what your past or even your present says about you. I don't care if you're petite or overweight, a CEO or an entry level employee. I don't care if all the cards seem stacked against you and that God couldn't possibly turn your pain or mess into a platform for His plan. He sees you. He loves you. You're not an orphan anymore, you're a son or daughter of God. And He wants to use all of you for such a time as this.

What do you have to do? Simply surrender your life to the God who loves you enough that He desires to create and work through you. This isn't a guilt trip, by the way. It's not as though we can single-handedly butcher God's plan through our disobedience. Sin always hurts us and others, but as Mordecai reminded his niece, God's purposes would be accomplished even without Esther's "yes." We aren't God and the weight of the world isn't on us.

Even Esther was human. Even after the fasting of her friends, she didn't immediately march into the throne room demanding that the king change his edict. No, she invited him to a dinner (that one I told you she'd never have asked to be at) where she promptly...asked him to another dinner.

I doubt the food was so delicious that she forgot why she planned the dinner. Clearly she wasn't really interested in a second awkward dinner with the man who wanted to kill her whole race. The woman stalled because she had a serious case of nerves. But in the end, by that second banquet with the king, she found the courage to live out the story God had written for her. She could have hidden and buried the influential gift God gave her, but instead she chose to invest it in faith.

Like Esther, when we step into God's promises, He wants to give us His courage to live out His story for us. When God called Joshua to step into the literal promised land, He left Him with this powerful word: "Have I not commanded you? Be strong and courageous. Do not be afraid; do not be discouraged, for the Lord your God will be with you wherever you go." (Joshua 1:9) We can be sure that if God is commanding and orchestrating our call, then we have nothing to fear because His presence is with us.

God desires Light to reach the ends of the earth, and He's invited each of us to join His mission. Will you remain silent? Or are you willing to surrender it all to God and let Him use your strengths and weaknesses alike for His purposes? That's faith. And that's what being a moon is all about.

## TURNING THE TIDE

After all my moon research I can never be a passive fan of the moon again. I'm probably going to end up with a giant lunar tattoo on my arm one day and joke with everyone about "mooning" them as I pull up my sleeve. Is that not funny? Ok, so maybe not. See, I'm glad I tested that joke here before using it in public. Whew, that would have been awkward.

One of the coolest things I learned about the moon is the way it creates tides on the earth. While the earth's gravity holds the moon in orbit around us, the moon is constantly pulling back with a gravitational force of its own. Though only a quarter the size of the Earth, the moon's incredible gravity is enough to literally pull our oceans into a bulge, creating the daily rhythm of earth's tides.

The high tides occur on the side closest to the moon where the pull is strongest, and on the side facing away from the moon, where the earth is being pulled in the opposite direction as it's ocean.

The sun's gravity also affects the earth's tides, but to a much lesser degree. The sun and moon once again play off of each other in the creation of tides. When the sun and moon are working at right angles, their gravitational pull cancels each other out to a degree, causing lower than usual tides. Conversely, the highest tides occur when the moon is in line with the sun and their combined gravity exerts a greater force on earth's oceans[1].

This whole time I've been telling you you're supposed to reflect God's light like a moon. But the truth is that a moon is meant for far more than mere light shining. That's too tame for us as powerful image bearers of God Himself.

Far beyond simply standing as a witness to God, He's created us to be bearers of the power of His Spirit. Paul refers to the Spirit living in us as the same Spirit that raised Christ from the dead. That's power.

As Christians, therefore, we're not meant to avoid the world or live among the staggering darkness with our Christian porch lights on, we're made to physically influence the darkness. In fact, we're made to subvert the lies of the Enemy with the truth of God's kingdom. We're made to move mountains, and alter tides.

Jesus came proclaiming that the kingdom of God is near, and He calls each of us to live in that realm. Though the Enemy may run this earth for now, he has no jurisdiction over God's kingdom. And God, in His masterful plan, found a way to insert His kingdom right into Enemy territory.

When Jesus prayed "your kingdom come, your will be done, on earth as it is in heaven," (Matthew 6:10) He was asking that God's kingdom actually overpower the Enemy's reign here and now. When we surrender to God instead of the world, we're choosing God's kingdom over the Enemy's.

Ephesians 6:12 says, "...our struggle is not against flesh and blood, but against the rulers, against the authorities, against the powers of this dark world and against the spiritual forces of evil in the heavenly realms."
The battle lines are drawn between God's kingdom and the world's. The more we learn to live like a moon, focused on God's face and His truth over us, the more we live out God's will on earth the way He intended.

Spoiler alert: God has already defeated every lie, every evil, every force of the enemy's darkness. Though we face the brokenness of a world waiting on full redemption, we've been given powerful weapons of influence over the darkness in the meantime.

Second Corinthians 10:3-5 says,

"For though we live in the world, we do not wage war as the world does. The weapons we fight with are not the weapons of the world. On the contrary, they have divine power to demolish strongholds. We demolish arguments and every pretension that sets itself up against the knowledge of God, and we take captive every thought to make it obedient to Christ."

Nothing that stands against Christ and His truth can prevail. Our weapons are stronger than the Enemy's. He fights with hatred, lies, and manipulation. But God's weapons are love, truth, and the blood of Jesus. There's nothing stronger. And as we act with those weapons, armed with God's Spirit in us, God can use us to alter the landscape of the world around us, spreading a kingdom that infuses this world with hope.

If you feel like your faith and impact are small, know that God can work in even the smallest places that you trust Him. In fact, Jesus says that His kingdom can start as small as a mustard seed, maybe the same seed-size faith you're clutching right now. But when that miniscule seed grows, it defies logic, laughing as it emerges from enemy soil to become a gift to the world around it. That's the power of reflecting God in this world.

God's Spirit creates a gravitational pull within us that draws the world to Himself. But we have to be in line with Him and His kingdom purposes. Just like a physical tide is decreased when the sun and moon are working against each other, our impact on the world naturally wanes when we're at odds with our Maker. When we're distracted from God, we fall back on the world's lies. It's much harder to influence the world away from those lies when we're following them ourselves.

But (and this is one of the most exciting buts I've ever written) when we live fully facing God and we're lined up with His truth, He can use us to create some massive tides that shift the world's thinking. God wants to influence the world through you. He wants to light up your generation. The best part is, He's already approved you, already planned His work through you, before you even lift a finger.

Your journey to being used by God simply begins with that mustard seed faith and the surrender of Esther. Of Mary. Of Paul and Abraham. And like them, that surrender may take you to places of influence that aren't as comfortable or safe as you'd like. Living out God's kingdom in broken earth means we're in a warzone and at times our shining may feel a lot more like loss than glamor. Living fully surrendered may even cost our life.

But Paul boldly states what surrender must eventually produce in all of us moons: "I eagerly expect and hope that I will in no way be ashamed, but will have sufficient courage so that now as always Christ will be exalted in my body, whether by life or by death. For to me, to live is Christ and to die is gain." (Philippians 1:20-21)

To die is gain? If we perish, we perish? You may be asking yourself, "I thought in surrendering we were supposed to shine. I thought giving up was going to result in God lighting up the world, and death doesn't really fit into that picture. How can death be gain for us moons?"

If that sounds like a depressing way to end a chapter...it is. You can take your complaint up with my editors. But the unsettling end to this chapter might be a good reason to finish this book and learn a final (positive!) lesson about being a moon.

# MOON UNIVERSITY
## Lesson Nine

**Star Lie #9**: God's kingdom can't exist in Enemy territory.

**Moon Truth #9**: When we're aligned with God, He causes His kingdom to reign in us and overcome the world.

Question 1: Have you ever been afraid of doing something for fear you might get a little too much glory? How might the parable of the talents relate to your life?

Question 2: Do you believe that the purposes God has for you are contingent on what YOU do or what HE does? God has plans for your life from before you were born; what does it look like to live like that's true?

Question 3: What does surrendered faith mean to you? Can you think of people you know who have lived out surrendered faith well?

Question 4: Have you ever thought of life as a spiritual battle? What does it mean that we have the power of Christ in us that can defeat the Enemy?

Question 5: Discuss the analogy of the moon's gravitational pull and our task as moon's to turn tides. What tides might God be asking you to influence? What might you need to give up (die to self) in order to step into God's plan?

# 10
# THE GLORIOUS DEATH OF A MOON

"The Lord will be king over the whole earth. On that day there will be one Lord, and his name the only name."
**-Zechariah 14:9**

"Lord, you establish peace for us; all that we have accomplished you have done for us."
**-Isaiah 26:12**

### HOPE BEYOND THE FADING FLOWERS

If I close my eyes I can still feel the smooth hand-me-down couch in my parents' living room where I first heard the shocking news: Heath Ledger was dead. I'd stayed up far later than usual binging on tv, and there on the bottom of the screen the breaking news scrolled past in the early morning hours. He'd just finished an amazing performance as the Joker in The Dark Knight. Not much older than I was, he was bursting with untapped potential. How could he be gone?

Many of you can remember similar celebrity deaths and the way your mind struggled to comprehend what you heard: Robin Williams, Carrie Fisher, Prince, Cory Monteith. Dead? But they were so bright- such stars!

Death always seems to catch me by surprise, as though I'd watched the same suspense movie on repeat and expected a different outcome each time. Yet even though all death feels wrong to us, don't we sometimes feel especially appalled when a celebrity dies?

They represent the maximum shine factor and worth in our minds. Like demi-gods, they seem gloriously outside of our normal human status. They're rich and famous and important; obviously the normal rules of life simply don't apply to them.

But we watch over and over again as death ignores their star-status, their wealth and prestige, and brings them to the same end as the regular guy. The me. The you. The death of a star is the chink in the armor of our world's value system.

Our inability to control our lives or avoid our mortality is a major flaw in chasing our worth as stars who must strive to maintain our value. Our star-focused culture tends to minimize the itty bitty problem of death. That's because the value system that has taught us that we're nothing if we don't shine doesn't offer a road map for post-mortem value.

It's like asking an airline agent if they'll roll your frequent flier miles over to your account in the afterlife: you're going to get awkward silence followed by nervous throat clearing and zero eye contact. In the same way, our culture is ill-prepared and squirrely about answering the question of how to make our significance last.

This reality can bring us to a frantic place of fear or it can open us up to brilliant clarity. If even celebrity stars can stack and save their light and glory only to leave it behind when they die, their light is perhaps less powerful and potent than we think. Being a star gives the illusion of burning bright for our generation, but it's mostly a self-focused light that quickly gives out when our physical bodies do.

So how is being a moon any different? It isn't until we picture our end that we truly ask ourselves some hard questions: Why does it matter if I shine at all? Will the things that I've done last or matter when I'm gone? Do I get to keep any of that glory with me when I go? How does God fit into all this?

Death and being out of control: it's not what I'd call a comfortable discussion. Maybe don't jump into it the first time you meet your new boss or your future mother-in-law. Yet as we wrestle and get our hands dirty in these questions, we might just find a peace that surprises us.

If we're living like stars, we'll believe that our value ends with death, and our glory has the same expiration date as our bodies. But when we live as God-seekers, as moons, our value is as permanent as our eternal God. First Peter 1:24-25 says, "All people are like grass, and all their glory is like the flowers of the field; the grass withers and the flowers fall, but the word of the Lord endures forever."

The verse acknowledges that we may be Black-eyed Susans that have already dropped a few petals. No, we won't live forever in these bodies. The glory we gather apart from Christ is not only a cheap lie, but we don't get to keep it when we leave this earth.

But please don't torch this book or use the paper to blow your nose in while you cry over our fading lights. Because the second part of the verse reminds us that there is something lasts forever: God's word.

If that sounds kind of anti-climactic and unrelated to how we're meant to shine, let me explain. We already talked about the amazing power of God's word. He is the living Word and whatever He speaks into existence is beyond promise, it's a covenant. This verse says that God's word will never fail, end, fade or tarnish. What He has spoken and established will never be shaken.

What does that mean for us? If God and His word are forever, then all his attributes and glory are forever. His love is eternal, which means our worth in Him is eternal. His kingdom will reign forever, culminating in a new heaven and new earth that will outlast this temporary habitat. And when we place our trust in Him, we will live with Him forever, which means our souls don't have an expiration date at all.

The ways that God has used us in His timeless narrative won't be lost or inconsequential. His light and love (that we're reflecting!) aren't exhaustible resources, nor will they ever be revoked. This has powerful implications for our worth and significance as moons: anything we've reflected of Him will absolutely never fade. Not even in death.

Death isn't something for us to fear, because it can't separate us from the love of God ever. Though our sin should have brought us death, God has overwritten our sin and freely given us eternal life in Him. We will experience death as pain and loss here on earth- it certainly wasn't God's ideal plan for His children. But when we face death head on and realize it has no power over our souls or our worth, we can finally live abundantly free.

The truth is, we're not in danger of losing an ounce of love, worth, or hope in death. But if we refuse to understand life as God-seeking moons through the lens of death, we're in danger of missing the point of living altogether.

## DIABETES AND DEATH

It would be a bit dramatic to say that every day is life or death for me, but life as a type 1 diabetic isn't a cake walk. (I really shouldn't even be talking about cake- that's definitely a diabetic no-no.) Those with a chronic condition know what it's like to shoulder a constant weight that you never get to take a vacation from. Every morning I'm acutely aware that I only made it through the night because of a small device stuck on my skin, delivering the insulin to my body that allows it to work as it should.

Perhaps you've had hair envy or wished your muscles were as buff as the guy bench pressing 400 at your gym. (If that's even a thing; I clearly only go to the gym never.) Well, I have pancreas jealousy. For the love, why can't my insulin-organ just be a little more like Jeff's or Rita's? You know...functional.

Some days are surprisingly easy, and I feel almost normal. I mean, I have my skinny mocha coffee and my miracle medical supplies. Some days my glucose numbers stay where they should be and nothing stressful happens with my medical equipment. Some days I sneak a little chocolate without throwing my body out of kilter. But other days are sobering reminders of how vulnerable life is with a broken body.

One such complicated day, I naively set off to Starbucks with a sermon to write and the optimism to take on the world. But when I arrived, my blood glucose numbers were creeping slowly up to 300mg/dl. In diabetes world, 100mg/dL would be roughly a perfect score and unfortunately anything higher than that doesn't equal bonus points.

Though I'd pumped plenty of insulin into my body to bring my levels back to normal, my body showed signs that I wasn't actually absorbing the insulin. Every once in a while this happens and it usually means I need to change the spot on my body where I attach my insulin pump because something is preventing the insulin from being absorbed. It could be a kinked tube or some scar tissue.

No big deal, I'd just slip into the bathroom discretely and find a fresh place to attach my pump. I change my pump site about three times a week, so at this point it's second nature to me. I stick my device onto my body and push a button that inserts a tiny tube underneath my skin to deliver the life-saving insulin to my blood. Then I monitor all the insulin I take with a little remote control. The medical advances are actually remarkable- it's like wearing an external pancreas.

Medical miracles aside, a public bathroom isn't the most ideal or sanitary place to have to change your medical equipment. I wish I could see a replay of myself trying desperately to open my pump case in a level place with no danger of being exposed to water or germs. Floor? Heavens no. Back of the toilet? Gah! That's an accident waiting to happen.

But apparently finding that nonexistent bacteria-free spot to rest my supplies was hardly my worst problem.

When I went to take the pump off of my leg, I realized I must have unwittingly put the thing on a vein or artery (your guess is as good as mine). As soon as I took the pump off, my leg was bleeding like crazy where my pump had been. Of course I didn't have a band aid with me, and I couldn't exactly run out of the Starbucks bathroom with my pants around my ankles to ask someone for a first aid kit. (And make that a Grande, please!)

So there I was, panic-blotting my leg with the rough bathroom paper towels, still trying to get my new pump on, while chill music, hip vibe Starbucks waited on the other side of the door. In the end, I wedged some paper towels discretely down my pants to avoid blood stains and stop the bleeding, put on my new pump and my poker face and emerged as though nothing had happened. *Nothing to see here, folks.* Minutes later I was typing out my sermon, sipping a sugar-free iced drink in the land of the seemingly carefree.

While it's not my classiest vulnerable moment, I have a growing collection of such out-of-control episodes that are changing my perspective on life. I imagine you have such a list of "perspective moments" from your own life. Maybe you've had a true life or death experience that shook you to your core. Maybe you struggle daily with long-term illness, depression, or crippling anxiety. Maybe you've experienced the death of a loved one, a kid that's battling addiction, a job that suddenly dropped out from underneath you or a financial pit you couldn't see out of.

Places like that have a way of reminding us of what was true all along but we'd rather not admit: that we aren't actually in control of our lives. (Which has some interesting implications for us if we're trying to be stars who control our own light.) Though unplanned and painful, these invaders snatch us up from our comfort and shake us out of the cruise control life we gravitate towards.

My life was certainly on autopilot at one time. I had good Christian parents who loved and served God and raised us well. Though we got into some tight circumstances, we never went without food or clothes or shelter or friends. I guess I thought that following God was supposed to be a blessed thing. Maybe if we just surrendered to Him in the right way at the right time He'd do some awesome super-shining through us. Wouldn't we be wearing cheesy grins all the time because God is good and we were serving Him?

But since my diagnosis of diabetes, I've intensely grappled with the idea of suffering, pain and even death. I don't know if other twenty or thirty somethings think about death much, but eight years ago it came onto my radar in a different way. I've wrestled with why God hasn't healed me, and I've cried out to Him with life and death urgency. And while I can hardly say all my encounters with this disease have been positive, I've found a strange wisdom that has sprouted up in the soil where my pancreas failed.

David cried out to God, "teach us to number our days, that we may gain a heart of wisdom." (Psalm 90:12) Walking in the vulnerability of a chronic disease has given me eyes to see that this life is so surprisingly short and out of our control. So I'm numbering my days differently. Yes God heals sometimes, but in this world we'll still have trouble and we'll still end with death. I'm just praying I don't go in a freak pump accident in a Starbucks bathroom.

What makes you number your days? Feel free to put this chapter down to contemplate your own life for a minute. I'm not asking an easy task of you, to probe into your own pieces of pain and loss. Maybe you'd find it easier to process with someone close to you. But I promise this will be worth it.

I've walked with friends who have gone through far more heart-wrenching things than my diabetes. I'm not trying to minimize or sugarcoat your experiences. Though our stories are so different, none of us really wants those difficult places. I don't know anyone personally who is asking God to give them more pain or more loss.

But instead of plunging us into abject depression, we can believe that the things in our lives that remind us of the crushing curse of death are the very things meant to propel us to live a life that defies death. 2 Corinthians 4:16-18 says,

> "Therefore we do not lose heart. Though outwardly we are wasting away, yet inwardly we are being renewed day by day. For our light and momentary troubles are achieving for us an eternal glory that far outweighs them all. So we fix our eyes not on what is seen, but on what is unseen, since what is seen is temporary, but what is unseen is eternal."

When we ignore death we live our lives as though all of our worth and glory were wrapped up in right here and now. But when we not only acknowledge death but embrace it for the comma it really is, our whole perspective on life changes.

Paul reminds us that all the pain is temporary and is helping to produce an "eternal glory" in us. God isn't just transforming us, but renewing us, and He's using our pain to keep us focused on what's eternal. Each taste of death on earth keeps us from placing our hope and worth in temporary things.

Author and pastor, Levi Lusko, is intimately acquainted with the horror of death. He and his wife reeled when Lenya, one of their four young daughters, died suddenly. Though he describes honestly the deep pain and grief their family still experiences, he also shares the ways God has used this tragedy as a powerful eternal lens through which he views his life.

In his book, *Through the Eyes of a Lion*, Lusko shares how God's Spirit is like an anchor connecting our here and now with Heaven. He writes,

> "Until we see Lenya in heaven, we are connected with her through the Holy Spirit. Through choosing to be filled with God's Spirit, we can feel the cord grow taut. Honoring Jesus and walking in the light reel it in. The more room we give the Spirit to come upon us and control our lives, and the more receptive we are to heaven's signal and guidance, the greater peace we will enjoy, and the stronger the pull of the rope connected to our Savior and those in heaven becomes.[1]"

In wrestling with his daughter's death, Levi and his family are choosing to act on what they believed all along: that death doesn't have the final word. Everything they do here on earth is connected, like a tethered anchor, to a very real heaven where their daughter is already enjoying God's presence. God, the Living Word, has written wisdom and life even where death was favored to win.

Think again to those areas of pain or vulnerability that are unique to you. Have those places in your life made you bitter and resentful of God and death? Have you treated those difficulties in your life as obstacles to a full life? Or have you learned, like Levi, to believe that God is truly using your current troubles to achieve a far greater glory?

I'm going to challenge you to do something incredibly hard but equally important: begin to ask God to reveal to you how He's using the broken places in your life to produce "an eternal glory that far outweighs them all." (2 Corinthians 4:17)

Lay all of your grief and pain and loss at the feet of the same Jesus who made you and values you with His life. And ask Him to show you how He wants to use those vulnerable and even painful things in your life to number your days and tether your soul more tightly to heaven and Himself.

This is the kind of challenge that makes the Enemy shudder. Because the minute you believe in a God big enough to use the broken edges of your life to write a brighter story, the Enemy doesn't have a leg to stand on. He can no longer hold us down with resentment and anger and make us play victims to negative circumstances.

If we begin actually seeking out what God is doing in our lives in the middle of the mess, we're learning to rest in an eternal perspective. If we can view even suffering as beauty in the making, the enemy's weapons start looking like our assets.

Unfortunately for check-list people like me, this isn't a one-day experiment. Asking God to show us the fruit of the trials in our lives will take time and humility. God probably won't spit out an exact list of all the beauty He's growing in you through you pain right this very second. Surrendering our pain to the God who writes beauty from ashes is a process, and it's something we must repeat daily. But as you give God your weakness and honesty, His Spirit will fill you with incredible hope, peace, and even joy.

Numbering our days sounds like a really morbid experiment invented by that guy who came up with a website that's supposed to tell you when you die. It certainly doesn't top my list of fun things to do on a Saturday. But for all of us who want to live and breathe for God and make an earth shattering change in our generation, we MUST be willing to see our lives through the lens of death. Until we have fully faced our end, we'll never know what true glory and shining are all about in the present.

## OUR GLORIOUS END

As we wrap up our moon lessons, I want to leave you with a renewed vision of God's eternal glory that far surpasses the flimsy glory humans can give us. In the end, God will create a new heaven and a new earth and His glory will still be at the center: "...the Lord God Almighty and the Lamb are its [the New Jerusalem's] temple. The city does not need the sun or the moon to shine on it, for the glory of God gives it light, and the Lamb is its lamp. The nations will walk by its light, and the kings of the earth will bring their splendor into it." (Revelation 21:22-24)

Here's the beautiful thing about hitching your wagon to God's glory-star: His glory isn't going anywhere. When we live our lives to honor God, laying any splendor or reflection of Him back at His feet, we'll find that the very glory we thought we gave up has followed us right into eternity. Any good work or fruit that God produced in us to reflect Him is like a secret investment account that not even death can tamper with.

This is why Jesus says to "store up for yourselves treasures in heaven, where moths and vermin do not destroy, and where thieves do not break in and steal." (Matthew 6:20) You can't take anything with you when you leave, but we can bank God's very own glory for eternity precisely by living to magnify God rather than ourselves.

God's insane grace sees us chasing after the world's glow-stick light and whimsically points to the Sun itself saying, "I've been saving something better for you. Come and share this Light instead."

And miracle of miracles, in addition to bringing us into the glory of His presence, God will go on to reward us with a "crown that will last forever" (1 Corinthians 9:25) for running our moon-reflecting race here on earth. How does that even make sense? In fact, in the end we won't actually care about owning the glory or light that we thought gave us significance because we will be so fully aware that it was never our light to begin with.

It reminds me of my senior year of high school when I was honored for helping put on a fundraising talent show for the National Honor Society. The talent-show had required hours of labor to screen potential performers, coordinate acts, and find the perfect emcee for transitions. After all the sweat that was poured into that event, someone certainly deserved to be honored.

Except, um, I wasn't the one who worked hard to put it together. I'd volunteered to help run the event, but I didn't even try to rearrange my work schedule to help with the auditions and set-up. I allowed others to do the work, and I showed up with too little too late, full of guilt, to help run intermission concessions.

So when they called my name at our awards ceremony in front of an auditorium of peers to accept an award that I knew very well I hadn't earned, I wanted to grab the mic and throw my prize to the people that I knew had poured their hearts into the talent show. That reward felt like a stolen jewel in my hands- I didn't want the glory because I knew it didn't belong to me.

Yet that is the picture of heaven and of being a moon that I will end with. We could spend our whole lives here trying to strive after glory and hoping to secure our worth and purpose for eternity. But once we taste death and pass into that heavenly realm, we're going to see all our reflected glory for what it is: absolutely not our own. And still God is going to richly reward us for our reflection of His purpose and light.

But then we're going to look at those jewels in that crown we longed for and back up into the face of the One who poured out His blood for us, who worked out His plan in us all along. And with the elders we will shake our heads and look at our reward in dismay as we realize, finally and fully, how our offering to God was simply surrendering our nothing. Yet God will have used our nothing to change tides and transform our dark world. Can you imagine?

We're going to cast down our crowns and the glory we thought we needed to make us valuable, and with all of heaven we will say to our Maker,

> "You are worthy, our Lord and God,
>     to receive glory and honor and power,
> for you created all things,
>     and by your will they were created
>     and have their being." (Rev. 4:11)

This brings us full circle: Our lives, our significance, our very being, are loaned to us for such a time as this, to fulfill God's purpose for us in our generation. The best we can do with the breath God has given is breathe it back out in praise. We don't need to create our own glory to be seen or needed or loved. The greatest glory we can experience here or in eternity is the sheer luminescence of God Himself.

We don't need to strive. We don't need to prove anything. We don't need to complete our to-do lists, fill out quotas for Christ, or make all the people around us happy. We don't have to be better-than someone else or compete for our value because God wants to use each of us together in weakness to reveal more of Himself. We can rest in Him and find a glory that mysteriously flourishes outside of our productivity and perfection, fame or fortune.

May this truth seep into our hearts afresh. May we not be driven to know success or fame but to know Jesus Himself. And in the end we will find that the shimmer we so longed for was really available to us all along: to simply be in the beautiful presence of the One who owns all the glory to begin with. So sit with Jesus. Let the power of His Spirit move you. Embrace the full and complete worth He gives you. Surrender to reflect His love and justice to a dark world. And watch as God uses His own light through you to teach others how to be a moon.

## MOON UNIVERSITY
### Lesson Ten

**Star Lie #10**: Death is the end of our works and worth.

**Moon Truth #10**: God's glory and every reflection of Him lasts forever.

Read the following passage:

"Since, then, you have been raised with Christ, set your hearts on things above, where Christ is, seated at the right hand of God. Set your minds on things above, not on earthly things. For you died, and your life is now hidden with Christ in God. When Christ, who is your life, appears, then you also will appear with him in glory." (Colossians 3:1-4)

Question 1: How does this passage sum up what it means to "be a moon" in this world?

Question 2: What are the vulnerable places in your life that teach you to number your days?

Question 3: Like Levi Lusko, how can your own places of pain anchor you to heaven and lead you to live a life that defies death?

Question 4: What does it mean to you that your glory is completely wrapped up in Christ and will be for eternity? How might this affect the way you live your life today?

Question 5: Have you ever gotten credit for something you didn't deserve? How did that make you feel? Discuss what it must be like to receive a crown from God simply for reflecting His own work.

Question 6: What moons in your life today desperately need to know their Light Source? What might it look like for you to share the Light you've found with them?

# END NOTES:

Chapter 4: Redefining Shining
1. Speak Up Conference (For Christian Writers/Speakers): https://www.speakupconference.com/

Chapter 5: Dark and Low: God's Version of Shining
1. Morris, Rob. "Why Love146" Page, Love146, 2002-17, https://love146.org/love-story/, Accessed July 2 2018
2. IBID
3. IBID

Chapter 7: Glory in Community
1. reNEW Writer's Retreat (For Christian Writers/Speakers): https://renewwriting.com

Chapter 8: Gifts: The Good, the Bad, and the Ugly
1. Myers & Briggs Foundation: https://www.myersbriggs.org/
2. Godin, Seth. Tribes: We Need You to Lead Us. (New York, NY: Penguin, 2008), 136
3. Christine Cain's abolitionist organization: http://www.a21.org/
4. Carol Kent's Story: http://carolkent.org/our-journey-with-jason/

Chapter 9: Turning the Tide
1. Cooley, Keith. Moon Tides: How The Moon Affects Ocean Tides. 2002, http://home.hiwaay.net/~krcool/Astro/moon/moontides/, Accessed July 4 2018

Chapter 10:
1. Lusko, Levi. Through the Eyes of a Lion: Facing Impossible Pain, Finding Incredible Power. (Thomas Nelson, 2015

# ABOUT THE AUTHOR

Carrye Burr sees the irony in writing an author bio at the end of a book about defining ourselves through God alone. But her social personality won't let her leave without a proper introduction:

As a pastor's kid, Carrye feels privileged to have grown up in a diversity of states and churches. Today, she lives in CT with her creative, architect husband of ten years, and their three kids through birth and foster adoption. Though they have no plans to move, Carrye still enjoys connecting with diverse people, churches, and groups.

Parenting is one of her greatest adventures, but has also revealed her imperfections, inability to control life, and her deep need for God's grace. She's pretty sure she knows less about parenting now than ever before.

When she's not chasing kids or finding low carb recipes for her type-1 diabetes, Carrye enjoys deep conversations, searching all the coffee shops for the best latte, and attending murder mystery parties whenever possible. She recently rediscovered karaoke and is accepting song suggestions for altos.

As a writer (author of *Gray Faith*) and speaker, Carrye strives to spark honest conversation through her own vulnerable stories and questions. Her heart is to help others experience God's presence for themselves. Carrye believes every story matters, and is excited to encourage new and hiding writers to be brave and share their work with others.

She loves her church family (www.cthope.com) and is grateful for the opportunities to speak there. She's also branching out to speak at events and conferences and would love to find out how she could serve your group!

To contact Carrye or follow her posts, visit her blog or Facebook page:

www.lesstobemore.org

www.facebook.com/lesstobemore/